MW00824909

Bookkeeping

A Guide to Bookkeeping for Beginners and Basic Accounting Principles along with What You Need to Know About Starting an LLC

© Copyright 2020

The contents of this book may not be reproduced, duplicated, or transmitted without direct written permission from the author.

Under no circumstances will any legal responsibility or blame be held against the publisher for any reparation, damages, or monetary loss due to the information herein, either directly or indirectly.

Legal Notice:

This book is copyright protected. This is only for personal use. You cannot amend, distribute, sell, use, quote, or paraphrase any part of the content within this book without the consent of the author.

Disclaimer Notice:

Please note the information within this document is for educational and entertainment purposes only. Every attempt has been made to provide accurate, up to date, and reliable information. No warranties of any kind are expressed or implied. Readers acknowledge that the author is not engaging in the rendering of legal, financial, medical, or professional advice. The content of this book has been derived from various sources. Please consult a licensed professional before attempting any techniques outlined in this book.

By reading this document, the reader agrees that under no circumstances is the author responsible for any losses, direct or indirect, which are incurred because of the use of the information within this document, including, but not limited to, —errors, omissions, or inaccuracies.

Contents

PART 1: BOOKKEEPING 1

INTRODUCTION 2

SECTION ONE: BOOKKEEPING BASICS 5

CHAPTER ONE: WHY BOOKKEEPING IS ESSENTIAL TO YOUR
BUSINESS.. 6

Understanding Bookkeeping 6

The Role of a Bookkeeper... 7

Bookkeeping Tasks.. 7

Why Bookkeeping is Important.. 8

Single-Entry vs. Double-Entry Bookkeeping 10

Basic Steps of Bookkeeping... 11

Wrapping it Up.. 13

CHAPTER TWO: BOOKKEEPING VS. ACCOUNTING 14

Deciphering the Similarities of Bookkeeping and Accounting........ 14

Bookkeeper Roles vs. Accountant Roles 16

Evolving Landscapes 18

Wrapping it Up.. 19

CHAPTER THREE: MANUAL VS COMPUTERIZED BOOKKEEPING..... 20

Deciphering the Basics.. 20

UNDERSTANDING MANUAL BOOKKEEPING METHODS 21

HOW MANUAL BOOKKEEPING WORKS 21

SOME COMMON ADVANTAGES OF BOOKKEEPING 22

DRAWBACKS OF MANUAL BOOKKEEPING SYSTEM 23

COMPUTERIZED BOOKKEEPING SYSTEMS 24

BENEFITS OF A COMPUTERIZED BOOKKEEPING SYSTEM 24

DRAWBACKS OF COMPUTERIZED BOOKKEEPING SYSTEMS 25

MANUAL BOOKKEEPING VS A COMPUTERIZED BOOKKEEPING SYSTEM 26

WRAPPING IT UP 27

CHAPTER FOUR: 9 TOOLS TO HELP YOU WITH BOOKKEEPING 29

WRAPPING IT UP 39

SECTION TWO: BOOKKEEPING AND ACCOUNTING PROCESSES 40

CHAPTER FIVE: YOUR SYSTEM SETUP 41

WHAT IS A BOOKKEEPING SYSTEM? 42

EXPLORING THE BASIC BOOKKEEPING SYSTEM SETUP 42

WRAPPING IT UP 47

CHAPTER SIX: RECORDING TRANSACTIONS 48

DOCUMENTING YOUR BUSINESS TRANSACTIONS 48

FINANCIAL RECORDS – EVERY BOOKKEEPER'S LINGO 49

WRAPPING IT UP 54

CHAPTER SEVEN: GENERAL LEDGER 55

TYPES OF LEDGERS 55

CREATING ENTRIES FOR THE LEDGER 57

WHY LEDGER ENTRIES ARE RELEVANT 59

WRAPPING IT UP 60

CHAPTER EIGHT: UNDERSTANDING THE ACCOUNTING
EQUATION 61

*THE ACCOUNTING EQUATION – YOUR SMALL BUSINESS QUICK BALANCING
MEASURE* 61

ASSETS AND LIABILITIES – A QUICK PRIMER FOR SMALL BUSINESSES 64

WRAPPING IT UP 65

CHAPTER NINE: THE BALANCE SHEET 67

Balance Sheet – A Snapshot of Your Business Finances 67

Wrapping it Up.. 79

CHAPTER TEN: THE INCOME STATEMENT 80

Income Statement – Your Business Financial Reporting Tool.......... 80

Wrapping it Up.. 87

CHAPTER ELEVEN: THE CASH BOOK AND CASH FLOW
STATEMENT 89

Cash Book – Your Cash Transaction Cookbook 89

Cash Account vs. Cash Flow Statement.. 92

Wrapping it Up.. 93

CHAPTER TWELVE: CLOSING YOUR BOOKS.............................. 95

Closing Your Books – What Does it Mean?.................................... 95

Wrapping it Up.. 101

CONCLUSION 103

APPENDIX: BOOKKEEPING AND ACCOUNTING TERMINOLOGY.... 105

RESOURCES 112

PART 2: LLC 116

INTRODUCTION 117

SECTION ONE: LLC BUSINESS ESSENTIALS............................... 119

CHAPTER ONE: WHAT IS AN LLC?... 120

Types of Business Structures 120

What is a Limited Liability Company? 123

Types of LLCs 125

CHAPTER TWO: IS AN LLC RIGHT FOR ME? 127

Limited liability Companies Compared to Corporations.................. 127

Advantages of an LLC Over Corporations 128

*Disadvantages of a Limited Liability Company Compared to a
Corporation* 129

LLCs Compared to Sole Proprietorship 130

Advantages of an LLC over Sole Proprietorship 131

*Disadvantages of an LLC Compared to a Sole Proprietorship
Business*... 134

LLCs Compared to Limited Partnerships 134

Advantages of a Limited Liability Company Over a Limited Partnership 135

CHAPTER THREE: LLC BUSINESS STRUCTURES AND OPTIONS 136

Types of LLCs 136

Key Considerations When Deciding Between a Single and Multi-Member LLC 140

CHAPTER FOUR: LLC TAXES EXPLAINED 144

SECTION TWO: FORMING YOUR LLC 147

CHAPTER FIVE: STARTING FROM SCRATCH OR CONVERTING? 148

Forming an LLC from Scratch - An Overview 149

Converting Your Current Company to a Limited Liability Company 150

Important Tax Considerations for Conversion to an LLC 155

CHAPTER SIX: NAMING YOUR COMPANY 157

Branding Considerations for Choosing an LLC Name 159

Marketing Considerations for Naming for your LLC 162

CHAPTER SEVEN: CREATING YOUR ARTICLES OF ORGANIZATION 164

What are the Articles of Organization? 164

The Process of Filing LLC Organizing Documents 165

What Next? 170

CHAPTER EIGHT: THE LLC OPERATING AGREEMENT 172

Why You Need an Operating Agreement 173

Overriding State Default Rules 174

What to Include in Your Operating Agreement 174

Basic Provisions of the Operating Agreement of a Limited Liability Company 175

Other Provisions of the Operating Agreement 177

SECTION THREE: OPERATING YOUR LLC 180

CHAPTER NINE: SETTING UP YOUR LLC ACCOUNTING 181

The General Ledger 183

Choosing Tax Treatment 184

CHAPTER TEN: STEPS FOR SETTING UP ACCOUNTING FOR AN LLC 185

ACCOUNTING METHODS 185

THE ACCOUNTING CYCLE 186

CHOOSING AN ACCOUNTING SYSTEM FOR YOUR BUSINESS 187

SETTING UP YOUR ACCOUNTING SYSTEM 188

OTHER BOOKKEEPING ITEMS 188

HOW TO HANDLE ACCOUNTING FOR YOUR BUSINESS 190

WRAPPING UP 191

CHAPTER ELEVEN: CREATING YOUR FINANCIAL STATEMENTS 192

CREATING A BALANCE SHEET 194

STEPS FOR PREPARING YOUR INCOME STATEMENT 195

ADMINISTRATIVE EXPENSES 196

STATEMENT OF RETAINED EARNINGS 197

*PREPARE CLOSING ENTRIES TO GET THE BOOKS READY FOR THE NEXT
ACCOUNTING PERIOD* 200

CHAPTER TWELVE: HOW TO FILE YOUR TAXES AS AN LLC 202

HOW ARE LLCS TAXED? 202

CHAPTER THIRTEEN: SETTING UP PAYROLL AND PAYING
YOURSELF 209

TYPES OF EMPLOYEES IN A LIMITED LIABILITY COMPANY 210

PAYROLL RESPONSIBILITIES OF THE EMPLOYER 210

MANDATORY EMPLOYER CONTRIBUTION 211

PAYING YOURSELF AS THE OWNER OF AN LLC 211

MEMBERS EARNING WAGES AS AN LLC EMPLOYEE 212

HOW TAXES ARE PAID FOR LLCS THAT PAY MEMBERS AS EMPLOYEES 212

MEMBERS THAT RECEIVE DISTRIBUTIONS FROM THE LLC PROFITS 213

CONCLUSION 216

GLOSSARY OF TERMS 218

COMMON IRS FORMS 223

Part 1: Bookkeeping

An Essential Guide to Bookkeeping for Beginners along with Basic Accounting Principles

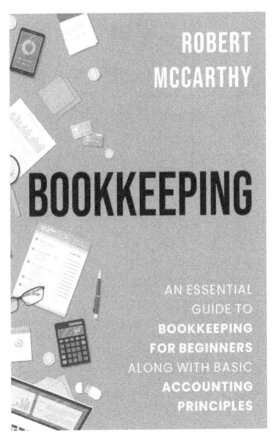

Introduction

Bookkeepers are the lifeblood of almost every business. If you believe that information is critical, you will agree that a bookkeeper has a crucial role in a company. The information recorded in books allows business owners to make essential decisions involving market strategy or product launches while handling several other financial aspects of their business simultaneously.

If it weren't for the ongoing efforts of bookkeepers, most businesses wouldn't know much of what was happening to their finances. With no precise financial knowledge, business executives would be merely guessing about the number of sales made, the cash drawings and withdrawals, or the cash that was paid out and the items sold to consumers during the year. It would be challenging to ascertain the amount paid out to employees or the amount spent on other business essentials.

Reliable and precise financial bookkeeping is essential to every business and is crucial to those who work within the company. Managers, owners, employees, and external teams like investors, lenders, and government agencies all rely heavily on the bookkeeper to record financial transactions accurately.

If you're an employee whose job is to keep the books for a small business owner, or you are a business owner who does the books yourself, your role is vital, and knowing the essentials of bookkeeping is paramount. Bookkeepers must be thorough, enjoy working with numbers, and be conscientious about inserting the numbers precisely into the records.

But here is another side of the coin: if you are new to bookkeeping, it might be challenging to navigate through these procedures. Well, here is the good news: this book walks you through all you need to know about bookkeeping.

What This Book Can Do for You

Bookkeeping is a continual process that starts with financial transactions. In this guide, we will cover:

- Documenting those transactions in journals
- Adding those transactions to a General Ledger
- Checking your books to ensure they are balanced
- Making appropriate changes or corrections where necessary
- Structuring financial reports to show how well the business is doing

Who This Book is For

If you picked up this book to get explicit knowledge of bookkeeping, I assume you are either:

- A business owner who would love to learn how to do your books. Most likely, you may have good knowledge of the market and its jargon, but you little understanding of bookkeeping and accounting,
- Someone who has already studied bookkeeping but is looking for a comprehensive 'refresher' or reference work,
- A staff member in a small business who has just been asked to take over a business's bookkeeping duties, and need to understand precisely how transactions are reported in the books, how to make sure that the entries are done correctly and accurately, and how to report financial information by using the data collected,
- Someone who does bookkeeping or intends to do bookkeeping for small businesses and wants to learn more

about how to set up and keep books. I assume you have a little knowledge of business terminology, but you don't know much about accounting or bookkeeping. Or, perhaps, finally,

- Someone going through a job/role transition where bookkeeping and accounting are vital skills.

This book serves as a quick starter guide. Hence, if you are entirely new to the world of bookkeeping, this book is for you. So, what are you waiting for? How about we kick-start your bookkeeping journey!

SECTION ONE: Bookkeeping Basics

Not sure of what bookkeeping is all about? In this part, discover…

➢ Why bookkeeping is an important business feature.

➢ How bookkeeping differs from accounting.

➢ Manual and computerized bookkeeping basics, and

➢ Some common bookkeeping software that can help you kick-start your bookkeeping journey.

Chapter One: Why Bookkeeping is Essential to Your Business

Most small business owners employ accountants to work for them. And guess what? The cost is often too high for a small business, so the businessman employs a bookkeeper who functions as the ears and eyes of the organization's accountant. The accountant assists the bookkeeper in establishing sound bookkeeping habits, and regularly reviews his or her work. The truth is that every small business owner wants to reduce costs while increasing their revenue, and doing the books yourself can help minimize your business costs.

Understanding Bookkeeping

Bookkeeping relates to managing and maintaining financial records like ledgers, reports, financial statements, income tax records, and more. Bookkeeping, also called record-keeping, is the accounting component that documents receipts, expenses, and some other business activities in the accounting system. Bookkeeping serves to provide the material required when creating financial statements. In other words, bookkeeping is the process through which data is placed into an accounting system. This can be achieved either manually on a physical ledger or digitally through accounting software like QuickBooks. While the benefits of bookkeeping are vast, it is a job that is often boring, difficult, and despised by many.

The Role of a Bookkeeper

Bookkeepers are responsible for maintaining a company's books that map out their financial transactions. Most bookkeepers depend largely on cost-effective tools to arrange and monitor information. A bookkeeper's primary duties can vary depending on the size and form of the business.

Bookkeeping Tasks

In essence, bookkeeping implies documenting and monitoring figures closely linked with the business's financial side. It is crucial for large and small businesses, but what exactly does it entail? The following are a few features of bookkeeping:

- Business Revenue and Expenditures: Bookkeeping tracks profits realized and expenses incurred by the company. Keeping records of business profits and expenditure is undoubtedly one of bookkeeping's core (and time-consuming) elements because it is the cornerstone on which all other bookkeeping and accounting practices are centered. Considering the importance of such records, and the possibility of human error, most businesses opt for computerized bookkeeping tools to lower the level of manual tracking required.
- Maintaining the General Ledger: A business general ledger serves as the framework of the data-collection process employed by accountants to archive and coordinate financial information used to produce financial statements for the company. It consists of a sub-ledger which may contain any number of journals.
- Keeping Track of Accounts Payable and Receivables: Accounts payable are the amounts of money your business

owes to retailers, manufacturers, government, etc. while accounts receivable is the money that your clients owe you for goods or services purchased.

- Handling Bank Reconciliations: One inevitable bookkeeping fact is that there are occasions in which the bank accounts barely corroborate the transfers reported. In such situations, reconciliations are required, which involve reconciling bank statements with bookkeeping documents and finding the cause of irregularities. Don't fret too much when you find yourself in such a scenario — trust me, it is nothing to worry about if you know the right procedure.

- Providing Financial Statements: As stated earlier, bookkeeping entails the preparation of financial statements like the following:

a. **Balance Sheet:** A balance sheet is simply defined as a report of a company's financial status. It essentially outlines the assets, liabilities, and equity of the owner(s) at a given date. Put simply, the balance sheet shows the net worth of the company.

b. **The Income Statement:** This is often called the profit and loss statement. It is a company management report showing the revenue, expenditures, and net earnings over a specific period.

c. **Cash Flow Statement:** Cash is everything. A cash flow statement is a measure of how funds are collected and spent within a given period. This is probably one of the most critical indicators for business owners, as it depicts the income you really make.

d. **The Statement of Changes in Equity:** Every business prepares this statement annually as part of the annual stockholders' report. For this reason, it is not regarded as a compulsory component of the monthly financial statements. This statement reconciles the equity of a business during an accounting period.

Why Bookkeeping is Important

Bookkeeping - the formal documentation and arrangement of a corporation's financial transactions - plays a vital role in the financial viability of any enterprise, but especially that of small business owners. A solid grasp of the finances empowers small business owners to make educated guesses and decreases the risk of misappropriating funds. Bookkeeping, financial statement preparation, cash flow management, and tax enforcement are inextricably related; detailed bookkeeping establishes a solid basis for interpretation and corroboration with the rest. The following are some essential benefits of bookkeeping that may explain why it is the most sought-after skill in small businesses.

- Professional Documentation: A detail-oriented and committed bookkeeper will, at all times, keep accurate and detailed records. This full documentation helps manage your business finances and is of great benefit if you need your financial statements — or when the company is audited — because the information is already in place.
- Bookkeeping Offers Crucial Insights into a Company's Overall Health: Bookkeeping helps businesses to generate financial statements that provide financial details and give a simple description of how the business is progressing. These reports enable you to monitor the cash inflow and outflow of the business (the cash that flows into the business and leaves the business at any given time). This is called a business's cash flow. Cash flow estimates are critical to attracting new investors and reassuring current ones. The ability to understand the financial performance of your business makes plans regarding recruiting, growth, and day-to-day activities simpler. Financial statements like your balance sheet provide you with essential facts for making critical business decisions from an objective viewpoint instead of taking chances.
- Bookkeeping Makes Tax Processing Less Difficult: When tax season comes around, and you have to provide your accountant with the appropriate paperwork to report corporate taxes, having clean records dramatically decreases the amount of time needed to file these tax forms. Instead of trawling through your company records, the accountant will

concentrate on identifying potential tax exemptions, saving time and essential business resources.

- Efficient Tax Compliance: Tax assessments are designed to evaluate the tax owed to Federal and local governments. Tax reports can only be completed when financial transactions are compiled. Efficient bookkeeping can keep tax matters in order and make it easier for companies to determine the actual amount of taxes owed. The information that has to be reported in tax returns must be correct and duly delivered. The inability to keep tax matters current will result in severe consequences including hefty fines and lawsuits. Bookkeeping plays a crucial role in presenting the correct details in a well-presented format and on a timely basis to avoid these fines and lawsuits.
- Bookkeeping Lowers the Discomfort of an Audit: Businesses run the risk of being audited at some time. It's not anything to look forward to, and planning for it is worthwhile. Getting your books coordinated and in one location makes it easier to present financial details at the right time, which will help prevent fines or unnecessary penalties.

Single-Entry vs. Double-Entry Bookkeeping

You will have to choose between single-entry and double-entry accounting when trying to set up your books. This is a problem that is sometimes daunting to many business owners, particularly those that do not have much expertise in bookkeeping and are looking to handle the books themselves. Single-entry bookkeeping means recording all corporate activities in a single ledger. This is exactly how most small businesses start, mainly because it is very simple to do. Double-entry accounting records any transaction as two transactions, reporting the sums as 'debits' and 'credits', and defines how the assets are moved into or out of an account. This depicts where your investments come from, and where they're heading.

Although double-entry accounting requires serious work, it offers a far more detailed view of a company's financial details.

Basic Steps of Bookkeeping

No doubt, bookkeeping tasks can be daunting sometimes, but a logical series of procedures will make bookkeeping easier. The following are some basic procedures of bookkeeping:

- Preparing Source Documents: The source documents are the reference point for bookkeeping operations. A company will receive a sales invoice from the manufacturer when it orders goods. If a company borrows money from the bank, it signs a promissory note, a copy of which the company retains. On the other hand, if a buyer uses a credit card to order a specific product or service, the company collects the credit card slip as validation of the sale. Each of these business forms serves as information sources that are inevitable in every bookkeeping procedure; in other words, they serve as essential details that the bookkeeper uses to document the financial impact of the company operations.
- Documenting the Financial Implication of Business Activity in Source Documents: Sales and purchases (transactions) have financial consequences that need to be documented; as a result of their consummation, the company becomes better off, worse off, or at least "indifferent." Other instances of business transactions affecting the company are hiring staff, making retail purchases, borrowing money from the bank, and purchasing direct-selling goods. The process of bookkeeping starts with the identification of pertinent details of each transaction. The Chief Accountant of the company sets out rules and methods to measure the financial implications of these transactions. Most likely, certain laws and procedures will be observed by the bookkeeper.
- Make Original Entries of Financial Transactions: Utilizing the source document(s) for each transaction, the bookkeeper

makes the initial entries into the journal and then into the company accounts. A journal is a systematic list of transactions in the order in which they occurred. An account is a different record, one regarding a specific type of business activity. Two or more accounts are influenced by one transaction. When recording a transaction, it is important that you employ the business's established chart(s) of accounts.

- Carry Out End-of-Period Operations: This is an essential step to maintaining updated accounting documents and making them available for the filing of management accounting reports, tax returns, and financial statements.

- Compiling the Adjusted Trial Balance for the Accountant: After all the end-of-period activities have been carried out, the bookkeeper collates a detailed rundown of all accounts, commonly known as the adjusted trial balance. Small and medium-sized businesses manage hundreds of accounts for their varying investments, liabilities, equity, profits, and expenditures. Larger companies hold thousands of accounts, while massive corporations can keep more than ten thousand accounts. On the other hand, tax returns, external financial statements, and internal accounting notes to executives contain a relatively limited number of accounts. For instance, the average external balance sheet documents just twenty-five to thirty accounts (perhaps even less), and the standard income tax return includes a relatively low number of accounts. The accounting officer will take the adjusted trial balance and merge related accounts into a summarized sum recorded in the financial statements or tax return. For instance, a business can hold hundreds of different inventory accounts, each included in the adjusted trial balance. These accounts are broken down by the accountant into one summarized inventory report, displayed in the company's official balance sheet. The accounting officer will adhere to defined financial reporting guidelines and income tax provisions when sorting the accounts.

- Closing the Books: 'Books' is the traditional word for a full collection of business accounts. A business transaction is a continuous flood of events that rarely stops precisely on the last day of the year, and will affect the preparation of annual statements and tax returns. The company will draw a simple distinct line between the operations for the just- concluded year (usually 12-month accounting period) and the preceding year by closing the books for the year and starting with new accounts for the following year.

Wrapping it Up

Let's face it! Bookkeeping is an integral part of every enterprise (small, medium, or large). Nevertheless, this accounting method is still ignored. Indeed, according to recent studies, some companies are unable to toe the mark due to poor financial reporting, inadequate accounting, or lack of accounting records/books at hand.

You now know precisely why bookkeeping is relevant. It could save you money, time, and unnecessary hassle. If you find yourself in need of a detailed bookkeeping procedure, this book essentially covers all that you need to know.

Chapter Two: Bookkeeping vs. Accounting

When most people talk of bookkeeping and accounting in the same breath, they are most likely hard-pressed to explain the difference between the two. Though bookkeepers and accountants share the same primary objectives, bookkeeping is more transactional and procedural, while accounting is more subjective.

In this chapter, we'll describe the basic similarities and differences between accounting and bookkeeping.

Deciphering the Similarities of Bookkeeping and Accounting

It is not easy for people with a non-commercial background to differentiate between accounting and bookkeeping; a novice may confuse the two terms. Technically, their functions and responsibilities rarely overlap, though both experts work closely to ensure that company records are correct and up-to-date, and the financial performance of the business is strictly monitored.

Here's a brief overview.

The Similarities
- Bookkeepers and accountants deal with financial details.
- They have the shared purpose of maintaining a business's financial well-being
- Their pursuits and expertise often intersect, especially in small companies.
- Basic accounting skills are necessary for both positions.

Differences Between Bookkeeping and Accounting
- Bookkeeping differs from accounting by definition. By definition, accounting collects, interprets, classifies, analyzes, and records reported financial data and transactions, and involves a high degree of subject expertise, analytical skills, and logical comprehension of the system. On the other hand, bookkeeping is a component of accounting that specializes in reporting the financial statements of a business in a structured manner. Hence, the role is administrative in nature.
- Requirement: Accounting requires specific expertise since procedures are more nuanced and systematic. Accountants with sufficient qualifications and knowledge typically rank as Certified Public Accountants (CPAs). However, bookkeeping does not require any specific training and qualifications to carry out the duties that fall under this heading. Bookkeepers only need to be well acquainted with the issues and protocols pertinent to their work, which is usually overseen by accountants.
- Goals and Objectives: As far as accounting is concerned, the goal is to analyze the company's financial condition and convey the details to the required authorities, including the shareholders. In bookkeeping, the goal is to keep track of all financial activities in the ledgers in a structured manner.
- Company Financial Process: Accounting entails capturing, measuring, classifying, reviewing, publishing, and summing up financial data. Bookkeeping is the method of recording and reporting financial transactions. Recording these financial

transactions is the very first key component and the substructure of the accounting system.

- Tools Employed: In bookkeeping, ledgers and journals are the essential tools. Accounting employs balance sheets, cash flow statements, and profit and loss accounts as its key resources.
- Types/Sub-areas: In accounting, planning of business budgets, schedules, and loan requests are often carried out via social responsibility accounting, management accounting, cost accounting, human capital accounting, and financial accounting. For bookkeeping, there are two common sub-areas: Single Entry and Double Entry Systems.
- Financial Status and Decision-Making: In accounting, a significant majority of the financial reports generated by the accountants explicitly demonstrate the company's financial status and can be utilized by management to make critical strategic decisions. An accountant captures the real financial picture of a business. They generally examine and analyze data, collate reports and financial statements, and prepare taxes. The bookkeeper takes care of the daily financial transactions of a business.

Bookkeeper Roles vs. Accountant Roles

Bookkeepers and accountants often perform the same job. Generally, the very first duty of a bookkeeper is to record transactions and keep you financially coordinated while accountants offer guidance, research, and advice on tax issues.

The bookkeeper diligently tracks receipts, sends invoices, manages payrolls, and assures that bills are paid on schedule. Often, since they are actively involved in the day-to-day operations of your company, they will offer more direct financial recommendations.

To use an apt analogy, consider bookkeeping as your routine oral care while accounting could be viewed as your annual visit to the dentist. If you invest a little time each day to care for your teeth, your dental appointment would be relatively painless.

You'll receive a quick check-up to make sure all is in order and will be sent on your way without any cavities or gingivitis.

Now, pretend that you have not been cleaning your teeth properly or flossing them. Having to deal with these cavities and inflamed gums could eventually cost you a lot in dental bills. You might have spared yourself a great deal of pain, time, and money by keeping things in order at regular intervals.

That's exactly the premise behind the function that accounting and bookkeeping play together in most businesses. Failure to look after the accounts may inevitably stack up work for the accountant by the end of the year. Bad bookkeeping also triggers small costs that accumulate over time. For instance, companies that do not keep track of monthly bills will eventually spend precious money on self-inflicted late fees. It's evident that a bookkeeper is essential. However, the real trick is to determine when to move from a part-time bookkeeper to a full-time bookkeeper.

Accountant or Bookkeeper – Which Does Your Business Need?

As a small business owner, you need your financial reports to be informative and reliable so that you can make sound investment choices while ensuring that you have a stable cash flow. As your company expands, as you take on more clients and suppliers, keeping track of how much money is going in and out of your company is complicated and time-consuming. Most small business owners make use of a computerized bookkeeping system, approved or employed by their accountant, transferring the financial details to the accountant on a weekly, monthly, or quarterly basis.

If you employ an accountant, a bookkeeper, or both, their eligibility needs to be established by asking for client feedback, reviewing certifications, or conducting screening tests. Bookkeepers are not always certified or licensed; their claim to such a position rests on their competency and skill level, qualities you will need if you, as the business owner, elect to do your own bookkeeping. The good thing is that this guide essentially covers everything you need to know about bookkeeping. Hence, you may not have to worry about employing a bookkeeper if you are a small business owner looking to save costs and maximize profit.

Evolving Landscapes

Accounting and bookkeeping have been in existence for a very long time, and these areas have undergone a vast degree of improvement in the way the procedures are carried out. This pattern will persist in the future. Some of the developments in bookkeeping and accounting in the near future may include the following:

- The Proliferation of Smartphones: More and more companies are moving their activities online, particularly as smartphones and mobile apps have become incredibly adaptive and easily accessible. Company owners tend to view data from anywhere in the world on several computers, and bookkeeping and accounting experts ensure that properly produced records are available online for their customers to download at all times.
- Broadening the Services: Newer innovations have encouraged accountants and bookkeepers to be open to technology developments while embracing new technical solutions. It is an avenue for bookkeepers to help their potential customers throughout this transition by providing value-added services like payroll processing, credit card reconciliation, and more.
- Integrating Accounting and Bookkeeping Functions: The distinction between accounting and bookkeeping is gradually disappearing. It is important to note that, with the introduction of accounting and bookkeeping technologies, certain aspects of accounting are progressively integrated into the bookkeeping process.
- Highly Effective Services: Consultancy and advisory firms are making good use of these emerging technologies and software and improving computational methods, making bookkeeping and tax planning business more productive and considerably cheaper.

Wrapping it Up

Properly managed financial reports by the bookkeeper, combined with a smart financial plan and accurate tax reporting by the accountant, ultimately increase the growth and, most importantly, the financial performance of a business. Some small company owners choose to handle their finances themselves. In contrast, others prefer to employ a professional so that they can concentrate on other aspects of their company that they genuinely enjoy. Whichever option you opt for, make sure it adds to your business growth rather than detracting from it.

Chapter Three: Manual vs Computerized Bookkeeping

Both manual and computerized bookkeeping methods are based on the same values, rules, and accounting standards. Business bookkeeping can be conducted with a physical, hard-copy ledger rather than with the help of a computer. But then, does that sound like a good idea? Tech supporters argue that software is a secure, more reliable, and stable means of performing any task. Comparing manual bookkeeping and computerized bookkeeping generally makes the software look like the best option.

Deciphering the Basics

How are you going to balance your finances? Will you get a pen and paper to start writing all the essential details, or do you utilize a computer? Surprisingly, business owners are asking themselves the very same question every day.

Like you, a business owner can decide to use a manual accounting system to manage its financial reports. In the same way, businesses also have the option of using a computerized accounting program to maintain their financial statements with the help of a computer and software program. How about we start by exploring the basics of a manual bookkeeping system?

Understanding Manual Bookkeeping Methods

A manual bookkeeping program can be put into operation easily. It's a basic form of bookkeeping that can function well enough for sole proprietors or small business owners. But what exactly does the process entail? The manual method is a bookkeeping system where records are compiled manually and without a computer program. Usually, transactions are published in papers, through which the details are carefully organized into a range of financial statements.

These systems have a high error rate and are sometimes slower than computer-controlled systems. Manual processes are most often used in small companies with few purchases. This is because new or small entities have fewer financial entries to produce, and perhaps their accounting needs are basic. Although errors are inevitable in a manual bookkeeping system, they can still be minimized and sometimes avoided as long as the person in charge of maintaining the financial records understands what he or she is supposed to do. When proper procedures are taken, manual bookkeeping can be just as reliable as the computerized accounting system.

How Manual Bookkeeping Works

The manual bookkeeping system is defined as any standard manual documentation of business operations to disclose the company's financial well-being to stakeholders, whether these stakeholders are employees, bank executives, or private owners. The systems are approximately divided into four rounds. These include Revenue, Purchase, Payroll, and General Journal.

Manual bookkeeping systems use physical documents, paper pads, and books. This is where all the transactions are recorded manually. Bookkeeping pages have four or more written columns and several rows, natural divisions for the details required, including date, definition, and dollar amounts. Journals and books consist of working and final versions of records and different books for the various accounts. Cash receipts could be one collection, for example, and payrolls could be another collection. The results of these working papers are generally merged into the general directory of the organization, which is commonly called the general ledger.

Some Common Advantages of Bookkeeping

Error Detection and Correction: Despite the simplicity and industry penetration of computer-based accounting systems, manual accounting also provides a range of upsides that make it a real alternative. The first one is the fact that it makes error correction very easy. Double-entry accounting, attributed to Luca Pacioli, an Italian of the 15th century, provides a simple means of avoiding mistakes in data entry and number conversion. Each transaction is performed as a debit in one account and a credit in another. Trial balances determine the equality of total debits and total credits. If this is not the case, a mistake has been made somewhere in the records.

Data System Failures and File Corruption are Minimized: Computer systems manage data in contexts that are not widely accepted by several users. Trying to open the wrong file with either the old data or having to face a data file with a digital error may destroy the applicability of your current data. Manual systems mitigate this by using a single file – the ledger – for each account.

Always Easy to Access: Electricity or Internet shutdowns won't keep you from operating on the accounts (unless you're plunged into total darkness.)

Data Entry Mistakes: Double-entry accounting in a manual system is labor-intensive since all transactions must be reported twice manually. Many business owners using a manual bookkeeping system employ a double-entry strategy, but most often, the second entry is generated automatically. While this does not preclude an incorrect number from being recorded, it does eradicate the dissimilarities in first and second entries.

Drawbacks of Manual Bookkeeping System

Possible Loss of Physical Copies: Though digital files can be corrupted, appropriate backups can secure records, even off-site copies, such as cloud service storage. Journals and books, being real objects, are vulnerable to destruction. Theft or fire may imply that all the financial data of a business is damaged or lost. Duplicating and processing the general ledger off-site can be a time-consuming process relative to other digital storage solutions.

Awareness of Accounting Processes: Unlike other consumer software or product, the Manual Accounting Program is not designed for ease of use; neither should you anticipate customer service or patented assistance. You may require a bookkeeper or accountant to set up and manage the manual accounting program.

There may be other drawbacks to the use of a manual bookkeeping system. Bookkeeping, for any company, can be a complicated task. A manual bookkeeping system requires you to grasp the accounting system to a degree that may be utterly pointless when dealing with a computerized system. This can be seen as an upside or a drawback, depending on the individual performing the accounting.

Often, a specially trained professional is needed to make sure that the business record keeping is carried out appropriately. Unraveling the complexities of the financial reports by hand can be tedious. As it takes a long time to accumulate reports, you might be ignoring other areas of the business and missing potential for growth. Human error also plays a vital role in incorrect financial records; manual bookkeeping can be monotonous and cumbersome, which may result in more errors from the accountant's end.

Computerized Bookkeeping Systems

Computerized bookkeeping systems can be defined as accounting systems that require a computer system and pre-packaged, customized, or configured accounting software. This system is based on the idea of a database. This database is regularly managed with an integrated framework where accounting technology applications and reporting mechanisms are used.

The two main components include the following:

- The Accounting System: A system of principles and a classification method for the maintenance of records.
- Operating Protocol: There is a standard approach or procedure for running the system. This is to ensure that the information is appropriately stored and processed. It includes a front-end interface, back-end storage, database management, and reporting system to store data in a database-oriented program.

Computerized bookkeeping benefits are based on velocity, precision, reliability, brevity, up-to-date information and reports, and much more. Let's take a moment to explore the pros and cons of a computerized bookkeeping system.

Benefits of a Computerized Bookkeeping System

- Precision: This accounting method is structured in such a way that it is precise down to the very minutest details. As the data enters the system, the software automatically performs all computations.
- Automation: Because all calculations are performed using software, computerized bookkeeping avoids the time-consuming procedures involved in manual accounting. For instance, as invoices are issued, they are stored immediately, making the bookkeeping process less time-consuming.

- Easy Data Access: With the use of accounting software, accessing accounting data outside of the office is much easier, especially if you are using online accounting.
- Reliability: Since the computations are so precise, computerized financial statements are extremely reliable.
- Scalability: The amount of accounting required not only increases but is more complicated as the business expands. All is kept clear in computerized bookkeeping, thus sifting through data with the help of software is more straightforward than sifting through a collection of documents.
- Speed: With the use of accounting tools, the whole process of account planning becomes faster. Additionally, statements and reports can be easily generated by clicking a button. Business executives need not wait hours or days to lay their hands on a significant report.
- Security: The latest information can be stored off-site. Hence, it is completely secure from natural and man-made disasters such as earthquakes, explosions, storms, bomb attacks, and much more. The program will be rapidly replicated on other machines in the event of a tragedy. Clever accounting takes that level of safety.

Drawbacks of Computerized Bookkeeping Systems

The key drawbacks of computerized systems revolve around the fact that they rely solely on the operating environment in which they function.

Some of them are:

- High Installation Fee: Computer hardware has to be replaced, and the software has to be updated once in a while with newer versions.
- Possible Fraud: Heavy reliance on computers occasionally contributes to more severe problems. With even more software data collected in the cloud, there is an increasing

possibility for hackers to access and exploit the financial details of your company. This puts the business resources in danger when hackers use employer tax identification to open credit cards and commercial loans. There is also a possibility that someone inside the company may have access to the records and engage in pilfering money from regular deposits and modifying the details in the system. Company owners must safeguard financial records carefully.

- Cost of Training: To guarantee the efficient and reliable use of the computerized accounting system, newer versions of hardware and software are implemented. This means proper training, and the cost of educating workers is incurred.

- Technical Glitches: Issues may emerge when dealing with computers. You could be compiling the monthly or yearly details and experience a power outage. Computers may become infected with a virus and may crash in the process. There is also the ability of users to inappropriately execute program functions with which they are not acquainted; if a user wants to do one thing but accidentally does another thing, it may take some time to fix.

- Wrong Details: The financial reports are only as reliable as the information entered into the system. Company owners who do not take the time to identify account categories can insert data and produce reports that are not reliable. Business owners will do a great deal to minimize the drawbacks and possible challenges involved with computerized accounting through proper preparation and program integration. Taking the time to do things right is faster and cheaper than struggling to get back on track when there is an issue.

Manual Bookkeeping vs a Computerized Bookkeeping System

No doubt, the computerized bookkeeping system has made significant progress in the field of financial management. But how exactly does it differ from a manual bookkeeping system? The following point briefly explains the differences between the two.

- By Definition: Manual Bookkeeping makes use of physical records and transaction books, to keep financial information. Computerized bookkeeping systems make use of accounting software to record business transactions digitally.
- Recording: In manual bookkeeping, the financial recording is done through the book of original entry or in an accounting book. Computerized bookkeeping, on the other hand, collates financial data using accounting software.
- Calculations: In a manual bookkeeping system, calculations are performed manually, while computerized bookkeeping systems take a more automated approach. In essence, only financial data inputs are required, upon which computations are performed within the computer system.
- Speed: Because the procedures of manual bookkeeping systems are quite tedious, the system is generally slow. The computerized bookkeeping system is comparatively faster.

Wrapping it Up

No doubt, the key to every successful business is to have an effective bookkeeping and accounting system. There are numerous ways to go about this, but you should go for the one that fits your business goal and objective. Small businesses can opt for a manual bookkeeping system where all computations are done manually. However, as the business increases in size, it is best to progress toward a computerized bookkeeping system where the processes are automated. Note: The goal here is to keep an accurate record of your finances.

Keeping an accurate record helps you to monitor your business performance effectively. Most businesses go for a computerized bookkeeping system, but a small fraction of small business owners still employ manual bookkeeping systems. Regardless of your decision, the choice of any bookkeeping system should be prompted by your business goal. You should consider your business needs before settling for any option.

Chapter Four: 9 Tools to Help you with Bookkeeping

Like every successful professional, bookkeepers can accumulate knowledge and use certain "tools" throughout their careers. This usually makes the job less complicated.

Good news! I've put together a list of the best bookkeeping and accounting software.

This chapter essentially walks you through some of these tools and shows how they can be employed in your business processes.

QuickBooks Online

If you are looking for the best accounting software worldwide, it's impossible not to consider QuickBooks Online. In QuickBooks Online, simplicity is the charm.

If you are a small business owner who detests the financial jargon and would much rather get on with the exciting part of becoming a businessman, QuickBooks Online should help you do just that. It provides a classic suite of accounting resources for almost anyone, including:

- Dashboards for the business's financial details and documents
- Financial reporting that you can configure to match your needs
- An invoice processor

- Digital bill receipts
- Payroll management
- The flexibility to convert payments into cataloged business expenditures.

QuickBooks Online syncs with a user's bank account and company credit cards to keep your business's financial records up to date. It is one of the most sought after bookkeeping and accounting software packages, thanks to its flexibility, numerous add-ons, project profitability, comprehensive payroll support, and extensibility. It is properly structured and has been tailored to meet the needs of the vast majority of users. But this does not mean that it's left with no drawbacks. QuickBooks Online is one of the most expensive bookkeeping tools for small business owners.

Sage Accounting

Like QuickBooks, Sage offers a range of accounting approaches aimed at helping companies simplify and improve their financial operations. Like QuickBooks, Sage provides the accounting applications in both mobile and web-based versions.

If you own a single-person business, then Sage Accounting Start will undoubtedly be at the top of your list. For example, you can report income and expenditures and make bank reconciliations for just $10 monthly.

Nevertheless, if you need extra features, you can easily upgrade, at a relatively low price of $25 per month — these additional features or functionalities provide a rundown of your business budgets, cash flow forecasts, and bill vendors.

Some features of Sage Accounting software:
- Fewer human errors.
- Saves time.
- Much cheaper than other bookkeeping and accounting software.
- Provides automatic backup to users with no form of additional charge.

- Gives users easy access to send invoices from the software to clients via email.

Understanding the Various Types of Sage Accounting Software

- Sage 50 Cloud Accounting: This is often priced on an annual subscription basis. It gives users the ability to add multiple users, which of course, incurs additional charges. Sage 50 cloud accounting is best suited to larger businesses.
- Sage Business Cloud Accounting: Sage business cloud computing focuses more on small businesses. It is cost-effective compared to other accounting software.
- Sage 200: This is best for business owners looking to manage supplies, business intelligence, and, more importantly, customers in a highly effective way. With this software, a small and medium-sized business can easily share vital details across their business teams and stakeholder groups.
- Sage Timeslips: Sage Timeslips is the perfect option for any business that provides invoices for products and services offered and would love to turn more employee time into revenue. Structured to streamline even the most complicated billing processes, Sage Timeslips provides all the details required to monitor time and cost reports, while generating invoices from such details.
- Sage Intacct: Sage Intacct is a cloud-based accounting and financial reporting tool built for almost any business size. It provides collaborative features and reporting functions that can be used to keep track of business finances.
- Sage 100cloud: This is a desktop-based application tailored towards supporting production, delivery, and utility organizations in handling their payroll, financial, and supply chain activities.
- Sage 300cloud: A desktop platform for handling billing, production, activities, delivery, banking, and much more through currencies and locations.
- Sage 500cloud: The most comprehensive Sage software system for large-scale market administration, including

accounting, banking, logistics, supply chain, production, automated accounts payable, and credit card processing resources.

Can the Sage Accounting tool work for you? Undoubtedly, that's for you to decide.

There is no argument, though; Sage falls short of all accounting software systems explicitly tailored toward supporting small businesses. While one of the Sage Business Cloud Accounting programs may serve very small companies, there are similar web-based, low-cost approaches that can fit properly. Moreover, while Sage 50cloud could be built in the style of QuickBooks Desktop, this approach is the best fit for larger businesses — with a high start-up cost of approximately $500 a year for the cheapest package.

Freshbooks

FreshBooks is one of the top brands when we talk about accounting software for small business owners and for a fair price. Although it started initially as an invoice and cost monitoring software platform, FreshBooks integrates with your bank statements to produce accurate financial records. It helps to manage your payroll and company payments while keeping track of your business timesheets.

Moreover, FreshBooks also provides integrations with a relatively lengthy list of common CRM and customer service applications, and you can broaden the features any time you need them. If you need natural, intuitive accounting software, FreshBooks may be for you. And just in case you get lost on the way, FreshBooks offers person-to-person customer support, free of charge.

Some Unique Features of FreshBooks

- An Easier Yet More Efficient Approach: The new edition of FreshBooks is quite easy to work, even though innovative technologies have been integrated into the software. A sleek interface now emerges with the software, and features to promote cooperation among teams are now present.

- Mobile Optimized: FreshBooks provides Smartphone extension for smartphones operating on Android and iOS. With this, customers can easily access their business information anytime.
- Digital Payment: The software's time monitoring feature is optimized for billing functions, which allows companies to get paid digitally through several payment gateways.
- Management of Billing History: The software hosts functionality that enables the monitoring of both old and recent invoices. Unpaid invoices can be deleted immediately using this feature.

Xero

If you love the unique features of QuickBooks Online and FreshBooks as possible accounting options for your small business, you might want to take a quick look at Xero. Xero, QuickBooks, and FreshBooks have several overlaps in terms of the accounting functionalities they provide.

You can expect the usual perks; financial summaries, intuitive dashboards, customized reports, invoice creation, payroll, business handling, and bank account synchronization. But Xero very much excels with its user leeway: unlike its competitors, Xero allows you to add as many users as you want, free of charge. If you run a small corporation with just a few employees (say one or two employees), this feature may not sound appealing or important. However, if the organization is on the broader side of the "small enterprise," then obviously, this should serve as a huge asset.

With Xero, you are assured of a quick and simple transfer from QuickBooks to Xero should you need it.

Some Standard Unique Features of Xero

- Easy to Set Up: You don't need to take hours or attend a series of training sessions to set up Xero. When all necessary data is added to the program, the app will take care of all purchases and contracts, all from a single page.

- Inventory and Asset Management: The software also serves as an inventory and asset management device, helping it to process and run payrolls and modify taxes for more than 20 countries. This can create detailed ownership records that can be used seamlessly with any purchase.
- Transactions Made Possible: Transaction types created by the program provide users with more productive transaction features. For instance, it is easy to customize purchasing files using ready-made templates created by Xero, which leads to more personalized documents.
- Accurate Financial Reporting: Xero provides financial statements that put the effects of all operations into one snapshot. Now, how is that possible? The software provides a dashboard display feature where business owners can easily track their cash inflow and outflow. This display feature offers easy links to essential parts of your accounts like expenses, bank accounts balances, and many others. With this, tracking payments and mitigating bookkeeping errors are made easy.

Sighted

Sighted seems to have all the interesting bookkeeping and accounting features that are important to small businesses, particularly sole proprietors and independent contractors. The software is beautifully structured for small business owners. Nevertheless, this is not to say that it is the best tool for small business owners, but if you are looking for cost-effective bookkeeping software for your small business, Sighted should do the job. It can be used to configure your invoices and quotes as well as track your business expenses and customer and supplier records. Sighted is worth thinking about for its efficiency, flexibility, and affordability.

Zoho Books

Zoho Books is a strategic accounting tool structured to handle the cash flow and budgets of small businesses. It is recognized for its unique ease of use. The product provides not only trouble-free accounting but also excellent service, uptime, and reliability. It is capable of delivering customized invoices to clients and even receiving payments online.

The software is not only useful but also efficient, allowing users total leverage over financial management. It has a variety of essential features, like Profit and Loss, cash flow statements, and balance sheet formation.

The dashboard is user-friendly and is capable of showing financial summaries and graphics. The system is also capable of simplifying certain back-office tasks.

Some Key Features of Zoho Books

- Quick Bank Feeds: Zoho Books imports all credit card and banking transactions, eradicating any need for manual data input. These details are also classified in compliance with the rules of the bank.
- Instant Notification of Transaction: Users can send messages to customers, advise clients to pay on time, and set a payment that is suitable for all parties.
- Customer Engagement: The collaborative functionality of Zoho books attracts more users by letting your clients know that they are part of the payment process. This is achieved by offering your clients easy access to their transaction estimates and invoices while enabling them to make direct payments online.
- Distribution and Tracking of Invoices: The software provides customized and recurring invoices. The program provides easy payment features. Offline transactions can also be captured and connected to specified invoices and tasks.
- Project Management and Analysis: With a mobile app or web platform, it handles multiple projects, adds tasks to every project, and delegates them to specific employees. Zoho Books can also estimate the costs incurred on projects by inputting the time spent on projects.

Plooto

Plooto is a digital payment and tracking system that combines Accounts Payable and Accounts Receivable optimization with leading accounting applications such as QuickBooks and Xero. If you are a small business owner looking to optimize your accounts receivable and payable process, this tool would be your best bet.

Small companies and financial experts can also benefit from the tool as it enables them to deliver sales invoices to customers and get paid faster with financial institution-grade protection. An important distinction between Plooto and other digital payment systems is that payments can be made even when the customer or supplier does not have a Plooto account. With their email address, funds can be sent directly and conveniently to their bank accounts, which also minimizes costly wire transfer fees and excessive charges. The deposits received and invoices sent are immediately reconciled and labeled as paid, making the procedure easier and less expensive. With Plooto, you can get rid of tiresome and stressful manual data-entry work, with the help of its incredible automation and strategic layout tools that can save your company endless hours. With Plooto, enhancing organization productivity is a must.

Plooto allows users to send payments from anywhere in the United States, Canada, and many other countries with favorable exchange rates.

Overview of Plooto Features

- Streamline Your Bookkeeping Procedure: Plooto speeds up your accounts payable and receivable procedures by placing your business decision-makers on a unified platform. With the help of automation and strategic workflow tools, it eradicates time-consuming and unnecessary manual data entry.

- Personalized Approval Process: Plooto allows for easy personalization of the approval process so that transfers can be checked and verified before any proceeds are processed. With only a few clicks, you can choose who can create, edit, and approve payments.

- Simplify Your Accounts Payable and Receivable Procedures: Regardless of your business objectives and process, Plooto can adjust to your individual need. Whether you are receiving a one-time payment from a new client, or a regular payment from an old client, Plooto offers an expansive range of payment methods, all on one platform.

Netsuite ERP

NetSuite provides a unique workaround for businesses focused on selling products online. The software integrates essential reporting tools like the ledger with eCommerce, distribution, and customer relationship management, to help the company expand. For example, it provides a customer representative that allows business owners to handle leads, automate correspondence, monitor sales, produce quotes, and coordinate calendars.

It provides an inventory tracking tool that keeps track of your business's stock, and a robust, streamlined dashboard that provides easy access to the performance metrics. It's usually accessible to any Smartphone. NetSuite ERP offers proven, robust financial management tools required to develop a complex and evolving business. This software takes your company beyond conventional accounting software by process optimization within the organization and gives you the insight you need to make smarter and faster actionable business decisions.

Common Features of Netsuite ERP

- Robust Financial Management and Reporting Tool: The vast majority of small businesses use NetSuite's financial reporting software system to handle their accounting and bookkeeping needs. It speeds up your financial closure, offers excellent expense management, transparent processes, and auditable revenue management that enhances the full real-time visibility of your business's financial viability.
- Modern and Completely Movable: If you have Internet access and a completely functional Smartphone or laptop, NetSuite can efficiently operate from any part of the world.

Bench Accounting

Although it's an interactive web app, Bench Accounting provides accounting and bookkeeping solutions and hires qualified teams to take care of your growing 'number-crunching' demands. With this, you can comfortably concentrate on other business activities that can contribute to your business revenue and overall business growth.

Working with Bench Accounting is a reasonably straightforward process. All you do is prepare your spreadsheets, invoices, receipts, and other business transaction data. You can upload these via a web app. The team delegated to your account will then classify transactions and consolidate payments with your banks, credit card, and even your PayPal account. Companies of various sizes can profit from the services offered by Bench Accounting. They have five-tier corporate rates, and they offer monthly and annual schedules to satisfy your accounting demands and budget constraints.

Features of Bench Accounting

- A Service and a Network: Bench Accounting takes the burden of coping with accounting and bookkeeping out of your hands. They appoint a team of experts to coordinate your financial data. Hence, the platform ensures that the information recorded is absolutely correct.
- Simple Process: Working with Bench Accounting is a fairly simple operation because you are only required to compile your invoices, receipts, and other financial details and send them off to the team of experts assigned to you.
- Web-Based Software: You don't need to send the records to Bench Accounting via mail and risk losing them. Instead, you can deliver them through an interactive web-based app, in which you can also view updates and messages from your allocated team.

Wrapping it Up

Let's face it. Regardless of how large or small your company is, you can save some time and resources from your financial reporting duties by integrating strategic accounting software.

If you can't stand managing payrolls and documenting employee expenses, or you want to handle the core finances of your company better, the accounting solutions discussed in this chapter should help. As a small business owner, each day is a valuable opportunity for you to expand and continue growing your business. You can employ these tools or software wisely to make the most out of your time. However, regardless of whatever bookkeeping and accounting software you opt for, always ensure that it suits your business goals and objectives.

SECTION TWO: Bookkeeping and Accounting Processes

This part introduces you to the bookkeeping and accounting procedure. Discover ...

- Step by step procedure for setting up your books.
- Processes associated with identifying and recording transactions.
- The basics of general ledger, types of journals, and procedures.
- The basics of the Accounting Equation.
- The nitty-gritty of a Balance Sheet.
- The essentials of an income statement and how to create one.
- The types and procedures associated with the cash book and cash flow statement.
- Step by step procedures on how to close your books.

Chapter Five: Your System Setup

For almost every small business, keeping track of all business and financial activities plays a vital role in creating a robust financial health base. Nevertheless, approximately 40-45% of small business owners agree that bookkeeping and tax planning are the hardest part of a business.

Close to 48% are put off by the financial cost, and 8% dislike all the paperwork involved in bookkeeping and accounting.

Despite the pain of handling business finances, the establishment of a basic accounting system is imperative to keeping detailed records that help ensure tax compliance, gauge cash flow, and make it much easier to attain sustained growth.

Basic bookkeeping can require loads of effort, regardless of how you decide to approach it (manually or digitally). Still, somehow, it keeps your financial records organized and structured, minimizing the likelihood of fund mismanagement.

This chapter walks you through the basic bookkeeping system setup, breaking down all necessary procedures to get your bookkeeping on the right track.

What is a Bookkeeping System?

Generally, bookkeeping systems are used to document your business's financial data and transactions. It typically includes running a general ledger, handling loan reconciliations, and keeping track of your accounts payable and receivable.

These details can be documented manually or digitally. The vast majority of businesses will opt for digital bookkeeping, which also leverages technology to reduce the more tiring facets of book management. Although the principle of transaction monitoring is clear, things can get messy; information needs, such as the operating plan or the scale of your company, affect the techniques you use for your bookkeeping system.

If you are new to bookkeeping and accounting in general, it could be pretty challenging to know how to start. Understanding the bookkeeping setup process provides a firm basis for even more nuanced yet useful financial statements and projections.

Exploring the Basic Bookkeeping System Setup

Rule 1: Choosing your Bookkeeping System

When setting up a new business's accounting system, you need to select a method for tracking transactions. There are two primary accounting methods: cash vs. accrual. Each approach utilizes a specific system to track income and expenditure.

Cash-Based Approach

I guess we should start with the simplest method – the cash-based approach. In a cash-based approach, you document transactions (revenue and expenses) when you earn and incur them. If a buyer pays you cash for a given commodity, you record it as a transaction. In the same way, you document your costs as you pay them. For example, you record the cost when you send a check to the retailer to pay for supplies. You report the profits as earned and the expenditures as billed. For instance, if you invoice a client for $5,000 on March 2nd and you received the payment on April 16th, you report this receipt in April; that's when you have the money in your pocket.

It is necessary to remember that this approach does not take into consideration any receivable or payable accounts. It refers exclusively to payments made and recorded at the time of payment, not the time of billing. Similarly, a cash-based approach only tracks the amount that flows out of the account when a payment is made to retailers, contractors, and other intermediaries. If you bought paper supplies on credit in May but did not pay the bill until June, you report the supplies as a June cost.

If your company earns annual revenue lower than $20-25 million, the cash-based accounting approach could be the right alternative. This accounting system is the best choice for very small companies like sole proprietorships or partnerships.

Accrual Accounting Approach

The accounting standard stipulated in the GAAP (Generally Accepted Accounting Principles) allows for accrual accounting for financial statements, which gives a better view of the company's financial standing. With the accrual accounting method, revenue and expenditures are documented when they are charged and earned, regardless of when the money exchanged hands. For instance, if a small company bills $500 in revenue on June 1st, you would report $500 in revenue on June 1st— even though payment was not received and the account not cleared until July 15th.

The same applies to your business expenses. If your small company purchases paper supplies on credit in July but doesn't pay the bill until August, you'd still report it as a July cost.

The accrual approach is more complicated than the cash-based method. You will have to use a double-entry accounting plan to report two entries for each transaction.

Each accounting system has its pros and cons. Most small businesses prefer to use the cash-based method, while others thrive more with accrual. Research both methods before choosing which one you would like to use for your business.

Rule 2: Decide How You are Going to Document your Financial Transactions

You have the right to decide how you would like to manage your financial transactions. There are generally three easy ways to go about this: hand recording, the use of accounting tools, or employing a bookkeeper or a basic accountant to do most of the work.

For small businesses, engaging a bookkeeper may appear too costly. Many businesspeople have resorted to hand-recording their day to day business transactions. The argument is that manual recording can take too long, not to mention the massive risk of error. If you have some money to spare, it's best to go for accounting software. It's computerized, so all you need to do is enter all the necessary business details. Also, you've got all your documents in one little machine.

Note, however, that having paper records of your purchases separate from automated ones will help, as these are a form of backup. If your computer crashes or you lose essential information on digital media, you can rest assured that you have quick and easy access to a backup of your files.

Rule 3: Select the Bookkeeping or Accounting Software That Best Suits Your Business Goals

If you choose to get the job done using accounting software, you may need to look for simple, low-cost, yet effective accounting software. There are several options open to you today, the most popular of which were covered in detail in Chapter Four.

Rule 4: Build a Chart of Accounts

A business's chart of accounts is a list of accounts based on their transaction classifications. You can allocate your transactions to a single account, or you can create a chart of accounts separated based on currency, sales, payroll, supplies, leases, salaries, accounts payable, and accounts receivable.

Your chart of accounts will depend on which accounting system you choose to use. For example, if you prefer to use an accrual accounting system, you may have to use a double-entry accounting system. Double-entry accounting is the most common approach used for small companies and other business organizations. There are two aspects of double-entry accounting, the first of which is that every transaction has two sides; one is credit while the other is a debit. The second aspect is that the transaction has two accounts. This bookkeeping system is used as an inventory, accounts payable, and accounts receivable. Double-entry accounting tracks your business finances and measures the organization's profit and loss account in a dynamic industry. That aside, double-entry allows for error-free accounts. And it makes sure that the company's actual position is shown in the financial statement.

This is not to say that a single-entry accounting system is not suitable for most businesses. A single-entry accounting system is going to work if you are running a very small business wherein its transactions are pretty small, straightforward, and do not require too much financial recording. Unlike a double-entry bookkeeping system, a single-entry bookkeeping system does not include accounts like accounts payable and accounts receivable. Like the name implies, every transaction in the record book is made in only one entry.

That being said, once you know how to create your business chart of accounts, you can use it to track all your company transactions.

Rule 5: Set up a Business Bank Account

Why do you think it is so necessary to differentiate your business funds from your personal funds? Here is a quick tip: having different bank accounts ensures that your records are accurate and streamlines your tax filing procedure. This is particularly essential when you contract an accountant to handle your taxes.

The records are meant to be reliable and real. If your personal funds are combined with the business fund, it will be hard to tell when there are glitches in the reports. Did you know that the vast majority of small business owners outsource tax preparations? This is exactly why you should have structured accounting records and separate bank accounts. Legally, companies and associations are allowed to have a different bank account for their business. While it is not mandatory for small companies, it is certainly encouraged.

That being said, you will have to register your business name with your province or state before you create a business bank account.

Rule 6: State Your Payment Conditions

It is important to state your payment conditions when setting up a bookkeeping system. In other words, you need to determine how you want to be paid. When revenue starts rolling in, you should have a payment plan in mind. For example, you can decide to opt for cash or go for credit card payments. Don't ignore the value of successful payment conditions for invoices. It dictates how fast you get paid.

If it takes forever to receive payment, your business cash flow may well be disrupted. This is exactly why an invoice is relevant. Ensure you have all the details that are required when a client makes a payment. They include your contact details, the number of items bought, and the due date for payments.

Rule 7: Set Up Accounting System Maintenance

Data collected and registered by your accounting system is essential to your company. Even if you use online bookkeeping systems, it is essential to set up a maintenance plan.

The first rule is to ensure the data is always entered correctly and promptly. Next, you must set aside a certain amount of time daily or weekly to record your financial transactions. You're going to have a smaller chance of errors, and you won't have a long list of further information to record.

Rule 8: Continuously Reassess your Bookkeeping Program

For new business owners, you should start with a basic spreadsheet when handling your business accounts. But, as the business expands, you should find sophisticated approaches and programs. As you begin to evolve, it's important to reassess your current framework. Evaluate the amount of time you spend when handling your accounts. It is also important to evaluate how much your bookkeeping needs cost. When you reassess and analyze your bookkeeping system now and then, you could perhaps switch from one bookkeeping system to another and save money.

The best bookkeeping approach implies that you are spending more time in dealing with your own business than on bookkeeping.

Rule 9: File it

File all documents, including your sales documents, payments, invoices, and paperwork. Business recordkeeping is a vital aspect of a profitable enterprise. File your company papers promptly. Initiate a day-to-day system for entering bills, expenditures, and other financial transactions.

Wrapping it Up

Setting up a business bookkeeping system can be an overwhelming and time-consuming task. When your company expands and your profits start rolling in, your accounting system will have to be more reliable. Note: The objective is to start right from the start. The trick to a good business is to make sure that everything is dealt with on schedule. The more prepared you are, the easier it is for you to handle your business affairs.

If the new accounting or bookkeeping system requires too much of your time, you may want to consider hiring an expert to assist with the task, or decide to use a computerized bookkeeping system. The bookkeeper is responsible for handling the day to day accounting statements, and is required to record every piece of necessary financial data and ensure that only accurate and up-to-date information is recorded. But this does not imply that you can't do your recordkeeping yourself.

Chapter Six: Recording Transactions

Bookkeeping involves recording all financial transactions; the major purpose of bookkeeping is to record all your company's financial records comprehensively, providing well-organized valuable information that can be used for further financial analysis.

Although exploring the essentials of bookkeeping is an important process, it is also important to consider those who will be using the records. Senior management may have dramatically different requirements to assess the company's success than the accountant who files and submits annual statements, multiple tax reports, and government remittances.

This chapter elaborates on the processes associated with identifying and recording transactions. Here, I will be providing examples and some essential best practices and tips when recording your financial transactions.

Documenting your Business Transactions

Every business owner needs to keep up-to-date records of their financial transactions. Whenever a business deal occurs, it should be documented in an organization book in one of various ways. The following outlines the most frequently used methods:

- Entries in a Journal: A journal entry is by far the most common approach used to document a transaction. Here, the bookkeeper manually computes the debits and credits alongside the account numbers for each transaction. This technique takes time and is susceptible to errors, and is thus generally reserved for modifications and special entries.

- Receipt of Invoices from Suppliers: In the bookkeeping cycle, when a bookkeeper receives an invoice from the supplier, the bookkeeper records the invoice into the accounts payable tab in your preferred bookkeeping software. This generates a journal entry that credits the accounts payable and debits the corresponding assets or expenditure account.

- Issuing an Invoice: When making an invoice for a client, the bookkeeper or the accountant in charge is expected to file the details into the software billing section. The module instantaneously generates a journal entry that credits the sales account and debits the account receivable or the cash account.

Financial Records – Every Bookkeeper's Lingo

Most businesses compile financial records such as retained income and cash flow, financial statements, and the company's balance sheet and tax returns. Keeping financial reports coordinated is a vital part of a profitable enterprise.

Although very few business owners start their businesses because they are big fans of documentation, it's a must to document your daily sales, purchases, and other transactions.

Monitoring your financial record starts with the correct reporting of transactions. Generally, as a business owner, you must keep an adequate record of the following:

Cash Account

In most cases, business transactions may be carried out through your cash account. Transactions may be split into cash received (debit to cash) and cash disbursements (credit to cash). When carrying out your monthly bookkeeping, you should update your bank statement with any pending expenses (for example, if you wrote a check, it ought to be recorded in your accounting records. The bank may not have cleared the payment on the same day and, if it is still outstanding by month's end, it should be showing as an outstanding check). Careful reconciliation of your financial transactions will compensate for the discrepancy between the dollar sums on the bank statement to the dollar amount in the accounting reports.

Accounts Payable

When a business orders products on credit, that transaction is recorded as an item in accounts payable (A.P.); this is classified as a liability and falls under the heading 'current liabilities.' Accounts Payable is a provisional debt obligation that has to be discharged to prevent debt.

Accounts Payable is a liability attributable to a specific creditor when ordering a given product or services without paying cash in advance; this implies that you have purchased products on credit. Individuals like you and I may also have accounts payable. We access electricity, Internet, wireless, and cable T.V. Expenses are incurred by the end of each month or a specific billing period. This implies that service was accepted, and must be paid for by a specific due date.

Now let's bring this down to a business perspective. Suppose company X purchased products from Company Y on credit. The cost of this product must be paid within 30 days.

Company Y will document the sale in accounts receivable, while Company X will document the purchase in accounts payable. This is simply because company X has to pay for the product purchased from company Y.

Accounts Receivable

Accounts Receivable (A.R.) is the earnings or payments that a business expects to receive from clients that purchased goods or services on credit. "Receivable" refers to the payment that has not yet been received. Accounts Receivable are classified as current assets in the balance sheet.

Let's use a broader example to explain this concept. Suppose your company, Smith and Sons Ltd, is a supplier of kids' toys. Now, let's assume a customer sends you an order for 1,000 toys at a total price of $10,000. When you issue the invoice, although the sale is reported, you may choose to offer the customer a 30-day credit period.

Until that specified due date, the amount of $10,000 will become part of your accounts receivable. When the payment is received, the cash section in the balance sheet will ramp up by $10,000, and the receivable will reduce by the same amount.

Inventory

The word inventory is often used to define the goods and materials held by a company for the primary goal of selling (or reselling) them. A business inventory may be raw, intermediate, or finished products.

Companies must select a system of inventory management. There are two basic ways to go about this: periodic or continuous inventory management. The continuous method allows the accounting documents to display the volume of inventory on hand at all times. It uses a separate account in the Ledger Subsidiary for each product in stock, and the account is modified almost every time a given quantity is added or removed.

In periodic inventory management, sales are recorded as they occur but inventory figures are not modified. The physical inventory will be taken at the end of the year.

Regardless of the inventory management system you decide to go for, it is safe enough to carry out a physical inventory on at least an annual basis, to ensure that the account records align with the actual inventory on hand.

When it comes to record-keeping, inventory itself should not be treated as an income statement of account. Inventory is an asset, and the final value will be listed as a current asset on the balance sheet. This is not to say that your inventory is not important when compiling your income statement. In fact, changes in a business inventory are part of the calculation used when defining the cost of goods sold, which is usually documented on the income statement.

Loans Payable

If any part of a business loan is still payable on the balance sheet date, the outstanding amount of the loan is called a loan payable. In other words, they are the amounts that have been loaned to your business.

These would also come from partners, friends, or relatives in small businesses. It is also necessary to be mindful of any interest that will be imposed on these loans.

Loans payable may be listed under existing or non-current liabilities, based on the duration of the loan repayment. For instance, if the debt was to be repaid within three years, the liability will be listed under non-current liabilities. After two years, it will be re-listed under current liabilities (i.e., when the loan is expected to be repaid within one year).

If the repayments were due in a series of intervals, the loan would be split into current and non-current parts. Both would be measured separately using a loan repayment plan.

Sales

Sales income, also known as revenue, is listed specifically on the income statement as net sales or sales. In its simplest terms, sales can be defined as the money received by a business in exchange for its goods or services.

In double-entry accounting, the sale of a product is outlined in the journal as a credit to sales and, on the other side, a debit to the cash account. The sum that ought to be reported is the real money value of the sale, not the selling price of the goods.

Maintaining Sales and Cash Receipts Journals

You can record your daily sales with your sales journal. It's best to keep a journal of combined sales and cash receipts to make your bookkeeping easier. For a journal that incorporates sales and cash receipts, you report both transactions, including credits, plus aggregation of accounts receivable, in one journal. This makes the whole record keeping process easy. The entries made in your cash and sales receipts should be extracted from the source document used to record your day to day transactions. These documents may include a daily sales register, cash sheets, and cash registers.

The data from each invoice is posted to an entry in the sales journal if you are using sales invoices. When managing your customer sales records, you must also add receivable ledger entries to the records to ensure that each customer record is constantly updated. Invoices for the sales should be labeled. Although paper copies can be stored in file cabinets, digitally updating your invoices makes better sense.

If you choose to make use of a manual bookkeeping system, prepare at least two copies; one for the client, and one for you. Ideally, the invoices should be prepared with three copies, with two versions that you keep; register one using the name of the client and the other by the number of the invoice. Include canceled or revoked invoices by their number before filing, so that you can account for them all.

The invoice should depict the following, whether it's manual or a computerized bookkeeping system:

- The day the sales were made.
- The quantity of goods bought.
- Price or value for money.
- An extension column (quantity multiplied by price) where applicable.
- The due date for payment.

You shouldn't worry about building a blueprint for sales invoices. Many office suites (like Microsoft Office or OpenOffice.org) provide a range of invoice designs that can be used to create your unique sales invoices as a starting point. A simple Google search for "sales invoices" would provide you with plenty of free templates to download.

Expenditures/Expenses

This account reports all costs accruing to the business. Costs can be categorized into broad categories, like office expenses, rent, and leases, or insurance as well as the cost of goods sold, which is measured based on the products bought and used during the year.

In a double-entry bookkeeping system, expenses are reported as a debit to the expenses account (that is, the income statement account) and a credit to either an assets or liabilities account. Expenditure lowers assets or raises liabilities. Buying a fixed asset, like a building or machinery, should not be treated as an expense or expenditure.

Wrapping it Up

Bookkeeping is about recording business transactions and keeping track of the financial health of a business. The goal is to record your business transactions in a detailed way that provides a snapshot of the company's financial strength. But this can only be possible if the appropriate strategies are employed. The strategies outlined in this book should walk you through this process.

Chapter Seven: General Ledger

In the early days, accountants and bookkeepers reported financial transactions manually, helped by a double-entry bookkeeping system. However, with the invention of computers, it became easier to monitor transactions at a glance. You no longer have to report in books; you can use advanced accounting tools and Excel sheets. Although both small and large businesses record transactions have evolved, the Ledger remains relevant. It is a vital accounting record for the production of financial results, which are critical to evaluating your business finances.

We're going to explore the fundamentals of a general ledger, explain how it works, and show why every business needs one.

Types of Ledgers

- Purchase Ledger: A Purchase Ledger is a ledger where the business organizes the purchases of goods and services from other businesses. It provides visibility on the amount charged by the supplier.
- Sales Ledger: A Sales Ledger is a ledger where the company tracks the sales of the items, supplies, or costs of the goods delivered to the buyers. The Sales Ledger indicates sales revenue alongside the income statement.

- General Ledger: A General Ledger is categorized into two types, namely a private Ledger and a Nominal Ledger. Nominal Ledgers contain information on costs, sales, depreciation, insurance, and much more. Private Ledgers, on the other hand, offer private records such as salaries, wages, capital, etc. Just like the name implies, a Private Ledger is not always accessible to just anyone.

General Ledger – Your Business Master Book!

Trust me when I say a general ledger is the master book of all businesses!

A general ledger is an accounting book that includes a comprehensive list of a business's financial dealings. This makes a quick peep into your business finances simple. It includes accounts like liabilities, fixed and current assets, income, investments, profits, and losses. This accounts book is perhaps the most valuable book for any company, so it is also known as the book of final entry.

Although the General Ledger is not the only resource you need when making business decisions, it will provide you with the information you need to analyze the business's financial results over the next month or the entire financial year. The General Ledger is an easy place to locate transactions that impact cash, inventory, Accounts Receivable, and any other account listed in the Chart of Accounts of your company.

A General Ledger is broken down into five different categories, known as accounts. They include the following:

➤ **Assets:** Assets are those resources owned by the organization which add value to the business. These may include cash, stock, accounts receivable, equipment, trademarks, and patents.

➤ **Liabilities:** Liabilities are existing or potential financial obligations which the company must pay. Current liabilities can include wages and taxes for workers, and non-current liabilities can also include items like bank loans or credit lines, as well as mortgages or rentals.

➤ **Equity:** Equity is simply defined as the difference between the value of a company's assets and its corporate liabilities. If a company seems to have more liabilities than its assets, it may have negative equity. Equity may include common shares, stock options, or stocks, which is strictly based on whether the owners and investors publicly or privately own the company.

➤ **Revenue:** Revenue is the company income that is generated from the sales of its goods and/or services. Revenue may include profits, royalties, dividends, or any other payments that the company receives from other companies or individuals.

➤ **Expenses:** Expenses consist of the money paid out by the company in exchange for goods or services. This can include rent, electricity, transportation, etc.

Generally, General Ledger will include a front page listing the names of the accounts described within, and this list is regarded as the "Chart of Accounts." However, the accounts documented within the General Ledger is known as the Accounts ledger.

Creating Entries for the Ledger

Since your business accounts are first reported in journals, you are expected to create several General Ledger entries which are generally dependent on the details pulled from the corresponding journal.

First, you report transactions in a journal, also called the book of original entry. Every line in this book is known as a journal entry. Entries may include items like dates, descriptions, and quantity of a product that has been purchased or sold. To stay organized, the journals are split into several accounts. You'll have five main accounts: assets, liabilities, equity, revenue, and expenses. These accounts can be further divided into smaller subcategories. For example, you can divide the assets into categories of inventories and receivables.

If you're using a double-entry bookkeeping system, you'll need to include a debit or credit. Debits and credits are entries that are similar but opposite. In essence, debits and credit account ultimately balance each other out. A double-entry bookkeeping system guarantees that the general directory of a business is always in balance. Each entry of a financial transaction in a ledger account debits that same account and credits the same amount elsewhere. For instance, if $2,000 were credited to the Assets Account Ledger, it would have to be debited in another account Ledger to reflect the transaction.

Debits and credits differently affect the accounts. Most accounts increase with debits, whereas others increase with credits. Let's see how debits and credits impact accounts, using the following bullet points:

- Revenue: Increased by credits and decreased by debits
- Assets: Increased by debits and decreased by credits
- Expenses: Increased by debits and decreased by credits
- Equity: Increased by credit and decreased by debits
- Liabilities: Increased by credit and decreased by debit.

After you have recorded the transactions in the journal, you can transfer them to General Ledger. You are expected to record every transaction in General Ledger, and, of course, these transactions are usually taken from the journal. When posting to General Ledger, provide the transaction sum and references to where the entries were initially entered in the books. This makes it easy for you to trace a transaction whenever a query arises. There will be times when you might wonder what a figure indicates. If you are a bookkeeper working for other businesses, your superiors or the business owner might question why some money was spent, or an auditor (an external accountant that checks for accuracy) could raise a query.

Regardless of the reason that someone doubts the entry to General Ledger, you certainly want to be able to locate the point of the original entry for each of these transactions in each account. This is where the reference information plays a vital role. It provides a quick direction as to where the initial transaction details can be found in the journals; this helps to answer any issue that may arise.

The General Ledger is a document of final entry. If you find it difficult to balance your accounts and estimate the gross values manually, you can do this in a jiffy by using basic accounting software which will automatically calculate the figures.

You can record your journal entries in a spreadsheet without having to employ bookkeeping and accounting tools. Even so, this approach may be time-consuming and may lead to further errors when posting to the Ledger.

As a small business owner, you are expected to update your General Ledger whenever you make transactions. Move journal entries to the Ledger at the end of each month. This document helps to organize the very same details in the journal, but this time, it is structured in a different format.

Why Ledger Entries are Relevant

We've outlined the basics of a general ledger, but you might be thinking, "So what? Do I need a ledger?"

It's really up to you (and, of course, your financial advisor) to determine what's best for your small company. You could be doing great without a general ledger, and for obvious reasons, you wouldn't want to spend unnecessarily! But if you're curious to know, there are several compelling reasons why you might want to consider using a general ledger for your small business.

Without a general ledger, you only have a list of unorganized transactions. Finding individual entries is challenging at times. Posting in the Ledger allows you to organize transactions, and general ledgers present a broad picture of your financial performance and evaluate your revenue and expenses.

Posting in a ledger makes it much easier to spot inconsistencies in the financial reports. Spotting these errors right on time is critical for accurate financial reporting and tax filings. In the case of an audit, learning to make up-to-date ledger entries will help you prevent unnecessary charges.

Wrapping it Up

Grasping and evaluating your company's accounting reports — like General Ledger — are necessary if you intend to boost your business and keep track of your financial situation. The effectiveness of a general ledger must never be underestimated. You need to understand how it works, how to generate the report, and what information can be gained from it.

The General Ledger is your master document for basically all financial transactions in your company.

You also need to grasp the basic concepts of double-entry accounting, the basic accounting equation, and how to move journal entries to the Ledger. When you understand and start using a general ledger, you will know how effective it is. It offers several powerful features. The most important, of course, is that it is the foundation for creating the financial statements critical to assessing your financial performance.

Consequently, given the importance of a general ledger, we would suggest using an accounting software platform to integrate your accounts, document your transactions, and manage your records. With the help of accounting software, you will minimize the risk of a manual error, create your general ledger instantly, and be able to develop additional reports that can be used for financial analysis. Also, accounting software will most certainly offer the ability to provide direct exposure to your accountant or business accountant so that they can help you track your financial activities within the system.

However, if you decide to keep your records manually, you may have to consider reviewing them regularly to ensure that all transactions reported are valid, up-to-date, and accurate.

Chapter Eight: Understanding the Accounting Equation

As a small business owner, it's important to understand your business's finances. One area you can look into is how much of your business assets are financed by debt as opposed to capital. Here is a quick tip – you can use the accounting equation to explore these basics.

It is almost tempting to neglect the term "accounting equation", especially if your small business employs a double-entry system. But what is an accounting equation, and why is it even important?

The Accounting Equation – Your Small Business Quick Balancing Measure

The accounting equation forms the basis of double-entry bookkeeping, a system in which financial transactions are recorded in two locations — one as a debit and the other as a credit. Although small businesses with few business activities can go for single-entry accounting, double-entry accounting helps to mitigate unnecessary errors.

The accounting equation is a simple description of the values entered on the balance sheet. This indicates the interaction between the assets of the business, the liabilities, and the shareholder or business owner's equity.

The accounting equation also indicates that any economic occurrence that impacts the balance sheet will also have a twin effect.

Generally, the equation can be expressed as:

Asset(s) = Liability (ies) + Owner's (or stockholder) Equity (ies)

The equation can as well be rewritten as follows:

Owner (or stockholder) Equity = Assets - Liabilities

Liabilities = Assets - Owner (or stockholder) Equity

The equation is broken down into three parts and their different underlying items: assets, liabilities, and equity.

Assets

Assets can simply be defined as those resources that your business possesses. Assets are often grouped into tangible assets and intangible assets. Tangible assets may include items like cash, receivables, inventories, machinery, land, and automobile, while intangible assets include copyrights, trademarks, and patents. They are located on the left side of a balance sheet.

There are two types of assets: current assets and fixed assets. Current assets are assets that can be easily transformed into cash. They include cash, accounts receivable, and inventories. The more current assets a small business has, the greater its chances of surviving and growing without borrowing funds. On the other hand, fixed assets are tangible assets that last more than a year and are of perceived value to a business. These may include assets like landed properties, computer equipment, and machinery.

Liabilities

Liabilities are all that a company owes, both now and in the future. It is usually located on the right side of the balance sheet. All companies have liabilities, unless they accept and pay in cash only. Cash involves physical cash or payments made via a company bank account.

Examples of business liabilities may include accounts payable, loans payable, wages and salary payable, income taxes payable, and interest payable.

There are two major types of liabilities: current and long-term liabilities. Current liabilities are also known as short-term loans. They must be repaid within one year and may include credit lines, loans, salaries, and accounts payable. A large variety of every business's expenses are current liabilities. These liabilities need to be closely monitored by the company to ensure that the company has adequate resources to satisfy such debts or obligations.

On the other hand, long-term liabilities that take a longer period to repay, such as mortgages and bonds. They are an essential part of the long-term funding of a business. Companies often take long-term debt to raise urgent capital to finance the acquisition of capital assets or to work on new capital projects. These liabilities are essential as they help to determine a business's long-term financial health. If businesses are unable to cover their long-term obligations, and these are due, the company is likely to experience a liquidity crisis.

There are also business liabilities that may occur depending on the outcome of a future event. These types of business liabilities are known as contingent liabilities and are sometimes called future liabilities. Consider this illustration: when a business is facing a $500,000 lawsuit, it will most likely incur liability if the lawsuit is successful. In the case that the lawsuit is not successful, the business will not incur such liability. In basic accounting principles, a contingent liability is reported only if the liability is probable (50 percent + likely to occur), and the size of the corresponding liability can be properly calculated.

But remember, liabilities are different from expenses. An 'expenses' item is the cost of operations that the business incurs to generate revenue. Unlike assets and liabilities, business expenses are closely linked to the business revenue, and both are included in the company's income statement. In fact, expenses are used to measure the net profit of business while liabilities, on the other hand, serve as an indicator of the company's credit status. For example, if a business incurred more expenses than the income it earned over the last three years, this could signal poor financial security since it has been making losses in the years under study.

Liabilities should not be mistaken for expenses. While one (expenses) is displayed on the company's income statement, the other (liability) is reported on its balance sheet. Expenses are simply defined as the cost incurred during the operational activities of the company, while liabilities are the obligations and debts that the company owes.

Assets and Liabilities – A Quick Primer for Small Businesses

Assets are what a corporation holds, and liabilities are what a firm owes. These are seen on the company's balance sheet, a financial statement that displays the company's financial stability. Assets minus liabilities equals the equity of the owner(s). According to the U.S Administration of Small Business, the assets of a business should be greater than its liabilities.

A business needs more assets than liabilities. With this, it has adequate funds (or things that can be easily turned into cash) to pay off its debts. When a small company has more liabilities than assets, it will not be able to cover its obligations and may be deemed insolvent.

Nevertheless, liabilities are not intrinsically harmful as they can be used in financing business growth; for instance, a line of credit is used to purchase new equipment for a small business. Such resources should help the business to work and expand, which is a positive thing. The key is to ensure that liabilities don't rise faster than assets.

Owner or Stockholder Equity

Equity has a range of accounting definitions:

- Equity may indicate ownership interest in a company, i.e., the equity of the shareholder or the equity of the owner.

- Equity can imply the value of the owner in a personal asset. For instance, the owner of a $300,000 house with a $25,000 mortgage loan should have $275,000 of equity in the property.
- Equity may indicate a mixture of liabilities and business owner's equity. For instance, the basic accounting equation Assets = Liabilities + Owner's Equity. If there are no liabilities, then it can be said that Assets = Equity.

The steps taken to measure shareholder equity are as follows:

- Identify the total assets of the company on the balance sheet for the year.
- Find the sum of all liabilities, which should be listed separately on the balance sheet.
- Identify the overall equity of the company and add the amount to the total liabilities.

Total assets must be equal to the sum of liabilities and total equity.

Owner's Equity or Stockholders' Equity indicates the portion of the company that a business owner owns. Simply put, stockholder's equity is given as the total assets of business minus its liabilities. It is used to represent the sums spent by business owners and the net profit of the company that has not been deducted or transferred to the shareholders. If the records kept by the business are accurate, the equation will be in a state of equilibrium, which implies that the two sides of the equation will be equal.

Wrapping it Up

The accounting equation is a straightforward way to analyze the interaction of financial activities across a business. In essence, it keeps track of the financial performance by filling in the equation's values, indicating that the equation is not designed for operational use. Instead, it is a concise explanation of how a company's financial side functions.

No doubt, the equation is a useful method for the double-entry system. This is because the equation ensures that the credits and debits side of a business book are captured accordingly. More so, it helps to determine the financial profitability of your business. The accounting equation is the baseline of the balance sheet. It presents a snapshot of the business liabilities, assets, and equity of the shareholder or owner.

Chapter Nine: The Balance Sheet

Periodically, you may want to know your business's financial position. Consequently, you are required to take a snapshot of your business status at the end of each financial year. This snapshot is called the balance sheet. It gives you a quick shot of your business status — how much you have in cash, how much you have in profits, how much you owe, and the amount invested into the business at a given point in time.

This chapter discusses the key elements of the balance sheet and how to pull these elements together to display your business's financial position in the best possible light. You'll also discover how to use certain analytical methods to see how well the company is doing.

Balance Sheet – A Snapshot of Your Business Finances

Generally speaking, a balance sheet provides a snapshot of your business's finances.

It is a financial statement of a business that contains, at the time of its compilation, assets, liabilities, equity capital, overall debt, etc. The balance sheet contains assets on the one hand and liabilities on the other. To ensure that the balance sheet reflects the actual image, all heads (Liabilities & Assets) must be reported (Assets = Liabilities + equity). The balance sheet is usually measured after each quarter, six months, or one year. Balance Sheets have two primary parts: assets and liabilities.

The balance sheet is split into two pieces or sections. The left side of the balance sheet summarizes all the assets of the company. To the right, the balance sheet shows the liabilities of the businesses and the equity of the shareholders. On either side, the mainline components are generally categorized as liquidity.

That said, the following are the basic procedures to prepare your balance sheet:

Gathering the Major Ingredients

The major ingredients of a balance sheet are the elements of an accounting equation. As a result, the balance sheet has three segments: assets (the business resources), liabilities (the obligations of the company), and the Owner's Equity (the investments of the owners and the revenue of the company). The details needed to complete the balance sheet can be located in the General Ledger of the business in which all financial transactions for a given time have been documented. Nevertheless, the following tips should guide you when working with an accounting equation.

The overall sum of the assets must be equivalent to the total liabilities and shareholder/ owner equity in the balance sheet.

The assets accounts depict all the goods and resources that the business owns. The liability segment of the balance sheet represents all the debts. The equity portion represents commitments from owners (shareholders) and past earnings. Technically, all a company's assets are either funded through debt, which is added to the liability accounts, or funded by past profits and equity-related contributions from investors.

Sort and Select the Balance Sheet Date

The balance sheet shall be drawn up to display the assets, liabilities, and equity of the company on a particular day of the year. Generally, businesses file a formal balance sheet quarterly (that is, the last day of March, June, September, and December) and at the close of their financial year (such as December 31).

You may not be able to complete the balance sheet until several days, weeks, or even months after the close of the fiscal year (e.g., December 31), but your data gathering date and balance sheet date may still be December 31.

Preparing the Balance Sheet Header

You can make use of the header "Balance Sheet" at the top of the page. Also, endeavor to outline the organization's name and the exact date of the balance sheet (the last day of the quarter or fiscal year).

Working on the Asset Section

The first component of your balance sheet is the Assets category.

An essential procedure is to split your business assets into two categories: current and long-term assets.

Current Assets

Current assets are those resources that your company owns. They can be easily converted into cash within one year of the balance sheet date. Current assets may include elements like cash, accounts receivable, and marketable securities (such as stocks, bonds, and inventories.) They are outlined in the order of relative liquidity, that is, how conveniently they can be liquidated.

Whenever cash is the first line of the items on a balance sheet, the account includes the amount you have on hand in the register and what you have in the bank (that is, savings accounts, money market accounts, and certificates of deposit.) However, you can simply outline this account as one item on the balance sheet – Cash.

A quick illustration:

The current assets of the company 'A.'

Cash - $5,000

Petty cash -$2,000

Inventory - $1,500

Accounts receivable - $3,000

Here, you can find the total of both cash and petty cash, which is $7,000, and list that amount on the balance sheet as a one-line item labeled 'Cash'.

Long Term/Non-Current Assets

Long-term, also known as non -current assets, are those resources that your business has which are expected to last for years. They are those assets that you are expected to have for more than twelve months. Long term assets encompass resources like land, buildings, facilities, furniture, cars, and everything else you'll likely have for more than a year.

The long-term assets of company 'A':

Equipment - $10,000

Fittings - $45,000

Vehicles -$30,000

Many businesses have more elements in the long-term assets of a balance sheet than those outlined above. For example, a production company may have several machines, plants, or fittings made specifically for its production processes. However, when a business employs a series of tools during its business procedures, these tools should be listed as a line item in the long-term asset segment of the balance sheet. Likewise, if your company owns one or more properties, you will have one line for land and buildings. Or, if you're renting a house with an option to buy a capitalized lease at a specific future date, it is considered a long-term asset and is classified as a capitalized lease on the balance sheet.

Some businesses rent out their office space and then spend a fortune to patch it up. For instance, a restaurant can rent out a large room and then furnish it according to the client's taste. The money spent on space-fixing is a long-term asset known as Leasehold upgrades and must be included in the Balance Sheet. It must be displayed in the long-term assets segment of the balance sheet.

All I have discussed in this section so far, ranging from land, buildings, capitalization leases, leasehold upgrades, etc., are tangible assets. They are those things you can feel or hold. Another long-term asset type is what accountants call intangible assets. Intangible assets are not physical objects; typical examples of such properties are patents, copyrights, and trademarks (all issued by the government).

- Patent Right: A Patent Right gives businesses the right to control patented markets. When a patent has expired, usually between 14 and 20 years after it was filed, competitors are permitted to join the market for the patented product, and the competition allows the buyers to lower their price. For example, pharmaceuticals patent their new drugs and are licensed as the sole suppliers of such products. When your doctor approves a brand name drug, you are getting a patented medicine. We also have generic drugs, which are those products that are out of patent; this implies that any pharmaceutical company can manufacture and distribute its variant of the very same commodity.

- Trademark: Trademarks grant businesses the right to distinguish names, logos, or designs as being their property. Trademarks can last indefinitely provided that the business in question continues to use the trademark and regularly file the required documents.

- Copyright: Copyright simply protects the original works, like books, journals, documents, newspapers, TV shows, films, music, poetry, and plays, from being replicated by someone else. This book, for instance, is copyrighted; hence no one can duplicate any of its contents without the author's permission.

To indicate the values of tangible and intangible assets being used in financial statements, all the long-term assets are either depreciated or amortized. The tangible assets of a business are depreciated, while a business's intangible assets like copyright and patents are amortized. Amortization and depreciation are quite similar. While depreciation involves the decreasing value of a company's fixed assets over the asset's useful life, amortization, on the other hand, focuses on spreading an intangible asset's cost over its useful life.

The life span of each intangible asset is determined by the number of years the government has assigned it. After an initial value is set for an intangible asset, it is measured by the corporation using the number of years it has government protection. However, the corresponding sum is written off every year as an Amortization Cost report on the company's income statement. Find the overall depreciation or amortization expenses that were written off on the balance sheet during the asset's lifetime in a line item termed 'accrued depreciation' or 'amortization' (depending on the one that suits the asset type).

Taking Account of your Debts

Liabilities appear right after the Assets section in the balance sheet. It reveals all the money your company owes to others, like banks, suppliers, contractors, or financial institutions. Just like the assets section on the balance sheet, you can split your liabilities into two broad groups. This may include:

- Long-Term Liabilities: These include those debts that you owe that can be paid over a period longer than a year. Payable mortgages, payable loans, and Bonds Payable are common accounts in the Balance sheet portion on long-term liabilities.
- Current Liabilities: Current liabilities are those expenses and obligations that you intend to pay for within the next twelve months. Some of the accounts that fall within this category include Credit Card Payable, Accounts Payable, and Current Liabilities, which includes business mortgages or loan payments due within the next 12 months.
- The vast majority of small and medium-sized businesses try to reduce their current liabilities because the interest rates on short-term loans, like credit cards, are extremely high when compared to those on longer-term loans. With this being the case, most businesses look for ways to reduce their interest costs by opting for longer-term loans with lower interest rates.

Listing your Investments

A vast majority of businesses have investors. Even a tiny family-owned grocery store needs money up front to keep the company on its feet. Also, in the balance sheet, investments are reflected as equity. The line items which show up in the Equity section of a balance sheet differ considerably depending on whether the business is incorporated or not.

However, when preparing the books of a business that is not incorporated, the equity section of your balance sheet is a bit unique; it generally contains the following accounts.

- Capital: The business capital is regarded as the amount of money or assets invested by the business owners when starting up a business. It also includes any further contributions made after the business start-up phase. If the business has more than one owner, the balance sheet should have a capital account for each owner to monitor their ownership share of the company.
- Drawing: This includes the money which the owners of the business took from the business. Balance sheets generally have a Drawing account for each owner to monitor individual quantities of the withdrawals.
- Retained Earnings: These are those proceeds that are reinvested into the business.

Equity for an Incorporated Company

On the other hand, the Equity section of the balance sheet for a company that is incorporated will include the following accounts:

- Stock: Parts of company capital, bought as investments by business owners.
- Retained Earnings: Retained earnings are profits invested back into the organization. To calculate the retained earnings of a business, start by finding the closing balance of retained earnings from the prior period (this can be located on the annual report). Next, add the net business earnings, which is given as revenue minus expenses from your Income

Statement, subtract the dividends distributed to shareholders, and then get the overall figure for current retained earnings.

This is given as retained earnings = ending balance of retained earnings from the previous period + net income - dividends paid to the company investors. The ending balance of retained earnings can be found in the company annual report, while the net income is found in the income statement.

Please note: The Retained Earnings will not be reported on the balance sheet, but can be used in estimating the value of the owners' equity.

Calculating the Owner's Equity

For an unincorporated business, the business owner's equity is made up of contributed capital (invested money), drawings, and retained earnings (historical amount of profit and loss). In contrast, for an incorporated business, company equity is made up of stock and retained earnings. Create a list of all the equity accounts such as common stock, treasury stock, and the amount of retained earnings. Depending on the type of business you are operating, once all the equity accounts have been listed, find the overall sum of all accounts and add the caption 'total owner equity.'

Pulling Together the Final Balance Sheet

After you have all your accounts grouped using the procedures addressed in this chapter, you should be able to produce a sheet of order. Most businesses in the United States typically choose between two common formats: the account format or the report format when preparing their balance sheet.

The exact line items that run in both formats are the same; however, the only difference here is how you set out the page details. The third choice, the Financial Position model, is more widely used in Europe, but just in case you ever come across it, I have explained it in this section.

Account Format

The Account format is a two-column model with one side of assets and conversely, liabilities and equity on the other side. The account format is somewhat a visual representation of the accounting equation. The assets are listed solely on the left. The liabilities are added together with the owner's equity and are reported on the right-hand side of the balance sheet. At the end of the list, both the left and right sides are totaled and should always be balanced per the accounting equation (assets = liabilities + shareholders/owner's ' equity).

Company A
Balance Sheet
As of December 31, 2020

Current Assets	Current Liabilities
Cash $4,000	Accounts Payable $2,500
Accounts Receivable $1,500	Total Current Liabilities $2,500
Inventory $1,000	Long-term Liabilities:
Total Current Assets $6,500	Loans Payable $35,100
Long-Term Assets:	Total L-T Liabilities $35,100
Equipment $6,000 Equity:	
Furniture $6,600 Capital $6,000	
Vehicles $30,000	
Retained Earnings $5,500	
Total Long-term Assets $42,600	Total Equity $11,500
Total Assets $49,100	Total L&E $49,100

Report format

The report format displays the assets, liabilities, and equity account in a vertical format. In other words, it is a one-column layout that shows the asset accounts, followed by the liability account, then the equity account of a business.

Company A
Balance Sheet
As of December 31, 2019
Current Assets:
Cash $4,000
Accounts Receivable $1,500
Inventory $1,000

Total Current Assets $6,500

Long-term Assets:

Equipment $6,000

Furniture $6,600

Vehicles $30,000

Total Long-Term Assets $42,600

Total Assets $49,100

Current Liabilities:

Accounts Payable $2,500

Total Current Liabilities $2,500

Long-term Liabilities:

Loans Payable $35,100

Total Long-Term Liabilities $35,100

Equity:

Capital $6,000

Retained Earnings $5,500

Total Equity $11,500

Total Liabilities and Equity $49,100

Financial Position Format

The Financial Position format, the third type of balance sheet format, is hardly ever used in the United States. However, it is widely employed in international markets, especially in Europe. This format has no Equity segment but contains two line elements that do not appear in the account or report formats.

- Working Capital: This is computed by subtracting current assets from current liabilities. It serves as an easy route when checking if a business has the cash available to pay their pay bills or not.
- Net Assets: The net assets of a business are those assets remaining after liabilities have been deducted from total assets. (Note that in the other two forms, Net Assets is equivalent to the Total Equity of a business.)

Company A

Balance Sheet

As of December 31, 2019
Current Assets:
Cash $4,000
Accounts Receivable $1,500
Inventory $1,000
Total Current Assets $6,500
Current Liabilities:
Accounts Payable $2,500
Total Current Liabilities $2,500
Working Capital $4,000
Noncurrent Assets:
Equipment $6,000
Furniture $6,600
Vehicles $30,000
Total Noncurrent Assets: $42,600
Total Assets less Current Liabilities $46,600
Long-term Liabilities:
Loans Payable $35,100
Fewer Long-term Liabilities $35,100
Net Assets $11,500

Working with Your Balance Sheet

You can evaluate specific ratios as well with a full balance sheet at your disposal by checking your cash position and monitoring your debt via a set of ratio measures.

Because these are the types of evaluations employed by most financial institutions to assess if it should lend or invest in a specific business, it's a smart move to do these tests on your own before applying for loans or investments. Ultimately, the ratio checks I will outline in this section will help you decide whether your company is in a good cash position.

Evaluating your Cash

Whenever you contact a bank or other financial institution to obtain a business loan, expect the lender to evaluate your cash flow using one of the two ratios: the current ratio and acid test ratio.

The Current Ratio and Acid Test Ratio

A current ratio is used to compare your current assets to your current liabilities. This offers a brief overview of a business's willingness to pay its bills. The formula to calculate the current ratio is as follows: current assets divided by current liabilities = current ratio.

Generally, lenders will look for current ratios between 1.2 and 2, and therefore any business with a Current Ratio of 1.5 should be considered a good deal. A current ratio below one is considered a danger sign since it indicates that the company does not have enough funds to pay its current bills. When the current ratio is above 2.0, it indicates that your business is not investing its assets properly and can make much better use of its current assets.

For example, if your business holds a lot of cash, you might want to invest that money in some long-term assets, like extra equipment that can help your business thrive. The assets part of this ratio does not exclude business inventory because it is not easily converted into cash when compared to other current assets.

Most financial institutions prefer the acid test to the current ratio when lending money to businesses because of its rigidity. Calculating the acid test ratio involves determining your quick assets (Cash + Accounts Receivable + Marketable Securities) and then dividing your quick assets by your business's current liability.

Most financial institutions consider businesses with an acid test ratio around one to be in good condition. An acid test ratio lower than one demonstrates that the business might have to sell some of its marketable securities or to assume additional debt until it can sell almost all of its inventory.

Evaluating your Debt

Before you can decide on when to incur extra debt or not, you should always evaluate the condition of your debt. The debt-to-equity ratio is one popular measure you can use to evaluate your company's debt status.

The debt-to-equity ratio is calculated by dividing your overall business debt (the sum of current liabilities and long-term liabilities) by its equity. Lenders prefer a company with a debt-to-equity ratio that is close to 1, as it shows that the value of the debts is equivalent to the shareholder/owner's equity. For example, a business with a debt-to-equity ratio of 3 might not receive a loan from loan firms unless the business debt level is reduced, or the owners pump more funds into the business.

Wrapping it Up

There are many reasons why the balance sheet is regarded as a key financial statement. It can be viewed alone and, in some cases, in conjunction with other statements such as income statements and cash flow statements to get a comprehensive picture of a business's financial status.

Potential investors, eager to learn what the business is worth, may like to see the balance sheet you file with the tax authorities if you apply for tax cuts or benefits. Of course, it also gives you valuable financial information on how the company is thriving. It demonstrates how the assets of a business are funded. If this is primarily through borrowing, then the value of the liability will be significantly high. If it's primarily through business owners' money, as is often the case for most businesses, then the equity figure will be higher. This serves as an important determinant during financial planning.

Chapter Ten: The Income Statement

Without a useful strategic reporting tool, it might be difficult to tell if your company made a profit or not. This technique is known as the income statement, and most business owners prepare this important reporting tool monthly, quarterly, or annually, to obtain a nearly constant snapshot of how well the business is performing financially.

Evaluating the income statement and the specifics behind it will disclose a wealth of information to help you make moves that are tailored toward increasing your earnings and overall business growth. This chapter discusses the importance of the income statement, how you can create one, and details on how you can use it to make informed investment decisions.

Income Statement – Your Business Financial Reporting Tool

How do I know if my business is making a profit or not? This simple answer can be found in your income statement, the financial report outlining all sales activities, costs of production or purchase of the products or services sold, and the costs incurred to achieve the business objectives.

The standard procedure would be to include three accounting periods in the income statement: the current period and the two previous periods. Thus, a monthly statement shows the current month plus the previous two months; for a quarterly statement, it shows the current quarter plus the two preceding quarters, while an annual statement shows the current year and the two preceding years. Providing all these details gives business owners and readers a snapshot of the earnings patterns of a company.

The income statement may have some variations between various entities because the expenses and profits may depend on the type of company or business carried out. Nevertheless, some generic line items are typically found in almost every income statement.

These five primary lines that make up an income statement may include:

- Sales or Revenue: This is the overall amount of money received from the sales of company goods or services. You measure this number through the combination of all sales or revenue accounts. The top line of the income statement would either be sales or revenues.
- Cost of Goods Sold: Cost of Goods Sold (COGS) is a line item that collates the actual costs of selling goods or providing services to generate revenue. It answers the question, "How much has been spent on the purchase or output of goods/services provided during the accounting period under investigation?" This line item is also known as the Cost of Sales if the business is a service provider. These actual or direct costs may include employees, supplies, and the distribution of other expenditures, like depreciation.
- Gross Profit: This is simply defined as the amount that a business has earned before taking into account operating expenses; it is measured by deducting the cost of goods sold from sales or revenue.

- Operating Expenses: Just like the name implies, operating expenses are the amount spent on business operations; these expenses include administration costs, wages, advertisement and promotional costs, utilities, and other expenses that are incurred during business operations. To get this value, you are expected to add up all the expenses in this category. In most cases, operating expenses are usually unique to businesses and industries since every business has a unique procedure.
- Net Gain or Loss: This is used to determine if a business made a profit or incurred a loss during the period under analysis. It is computed by deducting the overall expenses from gross profit.

Preparing the Income Statement

The income statement is just another term for the profit-and-loss account. This statement is essential for most businesses and, in fact, one of the three financial statements that business organizations commonly use. The other is the balance sheet (which we have taken time to address in chapter nine) and the cash flow statement. When preparing an income statement, small businesses ought to evaluate and document their revenues, expenses, and the subsequent profits or losses for a particular reporting period.

Income statements display the amount of profit earned by a company over a given reporting period and the expenditures incurred when generating revenue. The following steps should guide you on how to prepare an income statement.

Select your Reporting Period

The first step in planning and creating your income statement is to select the reporting date that your report will cover. Businesses usually choose to report their income statements on a yearly, quarterly, or monthly basis. Publicly traded firms are expected to file their income statements on a quarterly and annual basis. However, the case may be slightly different for small businesses, especially the very small businesses that have little business activity. As a small business owner, creating monthly income statements can help you determine trends in your earnings/profits and business expenses over time. This knowledge will help you make strategic decisions that are essential to your business productivity and growth.

Garner your Trial Balance Report

To produce an income statement, drafting, or printing a standard trial balance is an essential procedure. The trial balance could be easily produced from your cloud-based accounting software. In case you are wondering what a Trial Balance Report is, they are internal documents that display the final balance of every account in the general directory for a particular reporting period. It provides users with the final figures that are required when creating an income statement.

Calculate the Revenue

After the trial balance is set, you will need to compute your business's overall sales revenue for the reporting period under consideration. The income includes the amount earned for work during the reporting period, regardless of whether you've been fully r partly paid. Add up all elements in the revenue line from your trial balance report and include the total in the revenue line item in your income statement.

Finding the Net Sales

Net Sales is the sum of all sales minus any discounts offered to your customers. To determine the Net Sales of your business, look at line items for sales, discounts, and any sales expenses listed on your worksheet. For example, suppose your worksheet outlines total sales of $25,000 and $2,000 in discounts to customers, and according to your workbook, your business reimbursed $135 in credit card service charges on sales. You deduct discounts and credit card service charges from your total sales amount to calculate the net sales leaving you at $22,865.

Finding the Cost of Goods Sold

Your cost of goods sold may include items like direct labor, supplies, and overhead costs paid for the distribution of your products or services. Here, you are expected to add up all the cost-of-goods-sold line items, which may be displayed in your trial balance report. After this, you can input the total cost of goods sold on the income statement directly below the revenue line item.

In essence, the Cost of Goods Sold is the total amount that your company has spent on buying or making the goods or services that were sold to customers. To measure this amount for a business that purchases its finished goods from another business, you start by adding all purchases of new inventories to the opening inventory of the company and then deducting any closing inventory.

Note: The opening inventory is the amount in the inventory account at the beginning of a given accounting period, while the closing inventory is the inventory that's still on the store shelves or in the warehouse.

Since the cost of goods sold is given as goods available – closing inventory, for illustration purposes you can follow these procedures when calculating the cost of goods sold.

Suppose your business closing inventory, opening inventory, and purchases are given as $700, $200, $2000 respectively:

Opening Inventory at the beginning of the year+ Purchases = Goods Available for Sale

$200 + $2,000 = $2,200 (goods available for sale)

Goods Available for Sale – closing Inventory at the end of the year = Cost of Goods Sold

$2,200 – $700 = $1,500

Find the gross margin

Deduct the actual cost of goods sold from the overall sales on the income statement. This estimate will provide you with the gross margin or gross sum earned from the sales of your products and services.

Sum up the Operating Expenses

Sum up all the operating expenses stated on your trial balance report. Enter the total sum in the income statement as the element on the list of sales and operating expenses. This is situated just below the gross margin row.

Evaluate your Total/Pre-Tax Income

Deduct the selling and administrative expenses from the gross margin. This is going to give you a total of pre-tax income. Include this figure at the end of the income statement.

Calculate your Income Tax

To determine income tax, multiply your relevant state tax rate by your pre-tax income. Enter the figure obtained from your income statement below the pre-tax income statement.

Determine the Net Income

To calculate the net income of your business, deduct the income tax from the pre-tax income. Enter the estimate in the closing line item of your income statement.

Choosing your Income Statement Layout

Before creating an income statement for your business, you have to choose the layout of your financial details. You've two options to choose from: a single-step or multi-step setup. They contain the same content, but they deliver in entirely different ways.

The single-step format classifies all data into two categories: revenue and expenditures. The multi-step method splits the income statement into several parts and gives the reader some relevant sub-totals to make data analysis extremely easy.

The single-step layout enables individuals to evaluate the same subtotals as they occur in the multi-step layout, but these calculations involve more work for the reader. As a result, most organizations prefer using a multi-step to a single-step layout.

The income statement of company A, using a single-step layout:

Revenues

Net Sales xxx

Interest Income xxx

Total Revenue xxxx

Expenses

Costs of Goods Sold xxx

Depreciation xxx

Advertising xxx

Salaries xxx

Supplies xxx

Interest Expenses xxx

Total Expenses xxx

Net Income xxx

The income statement of company A, using a multi-step layout:

Revenues

Sales xxx

Cost of Goods Sold xxx

Gross Profit xxx

Operating Expenses

Depreciation xxx

Advertising xxx

Salaries xxx

Supplies xxx

Interest Expenses xxx

Total Operating Expenses xxx

Operating Income xxxx

Other Income

Interest Income $xxx

Total Income $xxxx

Finalizing the Income Statement

After calculating your Net Sales, Cost of Goods Sold, and the many other items outlined in the preceding sections, along with reconciling the figures from your trial balance, it is also important to finalize your income statement.

To finalize your statement of income, attach a header to the report that tags it a statement of income. Also, include the company information and the reporting period covered by the income statement.

Company A Income Statement for the year ending December 31, 2019

Sales $30,000

Cost of goods sold:

Material $3,000
Labor $4,000
Overhead $6,375
Total Cost of Goods Sold $13,375
Gross margin $16,625
Operating Expenses:
Advertising $1,500
Bank Service Charges $120
Insurance Expenses $100
Interest Expense $125
Legal & Accounting Fees $300
Office Expenses $250
Payroll Tax Expenses $350
Postage Expenses $75
Rent Expenses $800
Salaries $3,500
Supplies $300
Telephone Expenses $200
Utilities $255
Total Operating Expenses $7,875
Operating income $8,750
Income before tax $8,750
Income tax (at 30%) $6,125

Wrapping it Up

There is no limit to the number of internal reports that you can produce for the specifics that go into your income statement and other financial statements. For instance, several businesses are drawing up a report that looks at monthly patterns in sales, the cost of goods sold, and profits. In reality, you may decide to set up your accounting software (if you use one) to automatically produce this statement and other personalized reports.

You can generate these statements using your computer-based bookkeeping system at any specific time of the month, and you can assess how close you are to meeting your monthly, quarterly, or yearly goals. Many businesses may even draw up a report that compares actual expenditures to the business budget. Each item in such an income statement line appears with the corresponding planned budget estimates and the actual estimates. Just in case you are evaluating this report, you should take note of any line item that is significantly higher or lower than the projected value and, if possible, carry out research to come up with a reason for the discrepancy.

Chapter Eleven: The Cash Book and Cash Flow Statement

Cash book and cash flow statements are important in accounting and bookkeeping, as they serve as the essential asset of virtually every organization, be it a corporation, a government agency, a charity, or an academic institution. These books of accounting help to promote an organizational agenda, complete tasks, and lay the groundwork for greatness. There are loads of misconceptions surrounding these two reporting tools; one of them is that they can be used interchangeably.

This chapter provides sound protocols for controlling financial records, including cash books and cash flow statements.

Cash Book – Your Cash Transaction Cookbook

A cash book can be considered as a subset of the General Ledger, where all cash transactions made within a specific accounting period are reported in sequential order. Larger companies typically split the cash book into two sections: the cash receipt and cash disbursement journal. The cash receipts journal documents all cash earned by the business, while cash disbursements include all cash payments. The cash disbursement journal can include items like disbursements made to suppliers to minimize accounts payable. In contrast, the cash receipts journal can consist of items like payments made by consumers to accrued accounts receivable or cash sales.

Recording your Cash Transactions in a Cash Book

Basically, a cash book has two sides: a debit and a credit side. The business cash receipts are documented as debits, which appear on the left-hand side of the book, while all cash transfers are documented as credits, which appear on the right-hand side of the cash book.

The cash book is organized in columns. There are three different variants of the cash book: one column, two columns, and three columns. Cash payments and receipts are usually documented in the single-column cash book, and the double column Cash Book contains the business cash transfers and receipts alongside the details of the bank transactions. In contrast, the triple column cash book demonstrates those mentioned above but includes the purchase or sales discount details.

A standard single column cash book will have headers: the transaction date, a short narrative of the transaction, folio numbers, and transaction number. These headers are available on both sides, with the left-hand side displaying receipts while the right side displays cash payments.

Since the cash book is constantly updated, the transactions will most likely appear in sequential order. The accountant or bookkeeper in charge of the entry is expected to write a brief summary or narrative of the transaction in the description column. They also enter the account number for the relevant general ledger account in the reference or ledger folio column. The overall total of every transaction will be reported in the last column.

What is the Cash Flow Statement?

A cash flow statement is a financial statement that offers compiled statistics on all cash inflows that the business earns from its continuing activities and external investment streams. It also covers all cash outflows that were used in paying for business activities and expenditures over a specified timeframe.

The company's financial statements provide market participants with a snapshot of all transactions that go through the business, in which each transaction contributes to the growth of the business. The cash flow statement is assumed to be the most informative of all financial statements as it tracks the cash generated by the business in three key ways: through operations, investment, and financing. These three distinct sections of the cash flow statement can assist investors in evaluating the value of the company's stock or the company itself.

Sources of a Cash Flow Statement

The cash flow statement is not an alternative to the income statement or the balance sheet. It provides extensive details and identifies the reasons for alterations in cash and cash equivalents. The protocol for creating a cash flow statement is completely different from the process outlined when preparing the income statement and the balance sheet. However, the cash flow statement cannot occur in isolation; it is generally prepared with the help of financial statements like the balance sheet and the income statement.

That being said, the basic information required when preparing the cash flow statement may include the following:

- Comparative balance sheets at two time periods; that is, at the start and the end of an accounting period.
- The income statement for the current accounting period, and a few other handpicked necessary details for extracting hidden transactions.

Procedures for Preparing your Cash Flow Statement

Step 1: Calculate the net increases and decreases in cash and cash equivalents by comparing those accounts in the comparative balance sheets.

Step 2: Estimate the net cash flow from operating activities with the information in the profit and loss account, the balance sheet, and other relevant details. There are two ways of transforming net profits to net cash flows from financial activities: the Direct Method and the Indirect Method.

In the Direct method, the bookkeeper or accountant adds all the receipts and payments of the business. It is the widely preferred way to measure the cash flow since the recording of expenses and profits is so comprehensive.

The Indirect method, on the other hand, takes net income and then makes changes to reduce the impact of non-operating activities. This is regarded as an extremely easy strategy of calculating the cash flow statement when compared to the direct method, due to the obvious manner in which accounting departments generally record transactions.

Step 3: Estimate the net cash flow from investment activities.

Step 4: Estimate the net cash flow from your business financing activities.

Step 5: Prepare a structured cash flow statement detailing the net cash flow from (used in) operations, investments, and funding activities.

Step 6: Make an overall total of the net cash flow from the three activities. However, ensure that the overall net cash flow is equal to the net increases and decreases in cash and cash equivalents as computed in Step 1.

Step 7: Document major non-cash transactions that do not require cash or cash equivalents on a different schedule to the cash flow statement, e.g., purchase of equipment against the issue of share capital or redemption of debts in return for share capital.

Cash Account vs. Cash Flow Statement

Both cash flow and cash account are major catchwords in bookkeeping and accounting. Basically, both of them deal with cash receipts and payments. But what are the differences between the two? This section walks you through the major differences between the cash account and cash flow statement.

- Objective: The primary objective of the cash flow statement is to unveil both the cash outflow and inflow of a business, which is generally classified under operating activities, investing activities, and financing activities. On the other hand, the primary goal of a cash book is to capture all cash receipts and cash payments of the business, regardless of their nature, and to determine the cash balance at the end of the period under consideration.
- Period of Preparation: A cash book is prepared continually, whereby all cash transactions are sequentially documented based on when they occur, while a cash flow statement is a summarized description of the effects of those transactions, compiled from multiple sources, which is usually due by the end of a specific period (monthly, quarterly or yearly).
- Profitability and Liquidity: A cash book does not reveal the profitability and liquidity of a business. However, a cash flow statement highlights the profitability and throws light on the liquidity of the business.
- Cash and Non-Cash Items: A cash flow statement takes account of non-cash elements like write-offs of intangible assets, loss from the sales of assets, depreciation of fixed assets, etc. A cash book does not account for non-cash items; instead, the focus is exclusively on cash transactions.
- Decision Making: A cash flow statement serves as an effective tool for planning and controlling operations. On the other hand, a cash book cannot be used in planning and controlling business operations. But this is not to say that a cash book is not an important business recordkeeping tool; the book documents the business cash transactions but does not make business projections.

Wrapping it Up

Generally, a cash book documents the cash transactions of a company. In contrast, cash flow statements depict the amount flowing in and out of business, usually within a specified period. The cash flow statement does not only represent the amount of money flowing in and out of business; it also presents a quick run-down of what this income flow was used for. While both tools may differ completely in function, procedures, and many other ways, they work hand-in-hand to provide essential details that can be used to monitor your business's growth.

Chapter Twelve: Closing Your Books

'Closing the books' is a common task, and a decent bookkeeping system makes the experience fairly easy. Depending on your business type, this bookkeeping procedure consists of yearly or monthly transactions ensuring that the information recorded is properly classified. Fine-tuning of the entries must be executed with searches for errors.

More significantly, closing the books helps to properly account for your company's financial operations over the year. It displays your business finances in preparation for the next accounting period. New companies in their first year often encounter numerous obstacles at the time of closure due to lack of experience. That being said, strict adherence to the basic procedures outlined in this chapter will help to streamline this task. This chapter walks you through the basics of closing your books seamlessly and effortlessly.

Closing Your Books – What Does it Mean?

'Books' are a company's records of the business, and most importantly, financial transactions. These records are commonly used to generate reports which inform the business owners and investors on the amounts going in and out of their business.

In essence, closing the books indicates that these reports have been completed. These completed reports depict the financial position over a given accounting period – this might be monthly, or for a full year.

The closing process aims to ensure that profits or expenditures from the prior period are not carried forward to the current accounting period, making the estimates misleading. Closing your books annually enables you to develop and implement financial statements that provide all company owners with insight into the financial condition of their companies. Small businesses typically create statements like a balance sheet and an income statement at the end of the year to study and evaluate their business's financial status as they usher in the New Year.

Small business owners need to close their books at the end of the year to file their income tax returns. Closing books correctly always means that the accounting system is in working shape and produces correct statistics that can be included on the tax return. Most businesses also close their books monthly. This method is an effective way to perform monthly tasks such as balancing your bank statement, sending sales tax documents to the state, paying your vendors, and generating consumer statements.

Closing your Books – Your Year-end or Month-end Checklists

This section walks you through the basic procedures that are necessary when closing your books, specifically for a double-entry accounting system since this is the most prevalent method used by small businesses.

From the Journal to the Ledger

The journal serves as the very first takeoff pad for all your transactions. The process involves an analysis of business transactions to determine whether the transaction has a financial impact on the books of the business. This phase begins at the beginning of the accounting process and lasts for the entire period.

After entries have been recorded in the journal, the totals are moved to General Ledger. To close your books, report the amounts of your cash transactions to the appropriate general ledger account with your cash receipts and sales report. Cash payments include all payments made by cash, checks, or through online payment platforms. The same applies to your cash journal, but this time, the cash journal covers those funds that flow into the business and not the cash outflow.

Several small businesses close their books monthly, while others close their books on an annual basis. Closing your books monthly is pretty straight-forward; here, you are expected to include all transactions performed in a given month.

On the other hand, when closing your books annually, you are expected to select all entries spanning the year under consideration.

Summing Up Your Ledger Accounts

Yes, transferring your journal entries to your general ledger account is important, but it does not end there. You also need to find the total of each account in the ledger. The sum of each account serves as a pre-end balance.

Working Out Your Pre-Trial Balance

Next, the pre-end balance from the previous step will be used to create a temporary trial balance. This trial balance presents a quick shot of your business debits and credits at a glance.

A quick tip: The credits and debits must be equal. If they are not equal, there is a problem; you may have to do a thorough review of your books for errors. An easy way to go about this is by comparing and confirming these accounts balances with the help of third-party documents like invoices, receipts, and bank statements.

Adjusting for Unnoticed Transactions

Adjust those entries! Tracking those activities that are not recorded in your journal entries is essential; this is equally known as 'adjusting entries.' They are those entries that occur only at the end of the accounting period and can be used to account for any unnoticed revenue or expenditures for the year. They must be collated in the general ledger before they are transferred to the adjusted trial balance. For instance, if a transaction starts in one accounting period and finishes at a later date, an adjustment to the journal entry is necessary to better account for the transaction.

From the Adjusted Journal to the Trial Balance

The entries you made in your journal must be reflected in your trial balance!

After the adjusting entries have been made, these adjustments must also be recorded in the trial balance. This new trial balance is known as the adjusted trial balance – all debits and credits of a company accounts are recorded as they will appear on the financial statements. Here, you are expected to summarize your general ledger accounts once more to reflect the changed entries from the last stage. Next, find the sum; remember that the total value for credits and debits must be the same. If the values are different, review your books and, of course, update the necessary changes.

Working Out your Financial Statements

After you have adjusted your trial balance, you should be able to work out your financial statement.

For small businesses, in particular, the most commonly used financial statements are the income statement and the balance sheet. This is because most small business financing strategies are primarily done through loan financing, not through stock or shareholder equity.

Generating and preparing financial statements is perhaps one of the most critical phases in the accounting process. Such statements reflect the ultimate intent of the financial reporting system and the accounting system.

Preparing financial statements may be an easy or very complex process depending on the size of the business involved, as well as the business specifications. Such reports can be produced automatically through your accounting software. They provide an analysis of the company's financial condition at the close of the relevant accounting period, regardless of the period under consideration. Generally, they are compiled by the organization's accountant. But you can always decide to organize your financial statement with the help of bookkeeping/accounting software.

Compiling Your Closing Entries

If you are wondering what a closing entry is all about, this should explain it. A closing entry is a journal entry made at the end of the accounting period to switch balances from a temporary account to a permanent account.

Accounts Affected by Closing Entries

Closing entries can affect the following accounts:

- Revenue account
- Expenses accounts
- Dividend accounts

These accounts are temporary, or "nominal" accounts zeroed when closing entries are applied to an accounting system. Closing entries will reset these accounts so that they do not influence the next accounting period. Accounts are not erased; rather, their balances are moved to retained earnings, which is regarded as a permanent account.

Most businesses use the closing entries to adjust the balances of their temporary accounts, which display balances for a single accounting period, to a null value. In so doing, the company transfers these funds into permanent balance sheet accounts. These permanent accounts depict the company's long-standing finances. Let's take a moment to explore what these two types of closing entries entail.

- Temporary Accounts: Temporary accounts are general ledger accounts used to record expenses over a single accounting period. The balance of these accounts will eventually be used to create the statement of revenue at the end of the financial year.
- Permanent Account: On the other hand, permanent accounts are records that display a company's long-standing financial status. Balance sheet accounts, for example, are also known as

fixed accounts. Such accounts carry their balance forward during several accounting periods.

Please Take Note: Closing entries are only intended for a temporary account, while permanent accounts will never be closed.

Closing your entry (ies) – Basic procedures

- Close your business income accounts to the Income Summary
- Your expenses or expenditures accounts are equally important. Hence, ensure you close all expense accounts to Income Summary.
- Close the Income Summary of the required capital account
- Close withdrawals made to the capital account(s)

The procedures mentioned above are for small business owners like sole proprietorships and partnerships.

After these processes, zero out the income and expense accounts using closing entries. Closing entries will move the balance of these temporary accounts to permanent accounts. For example, the revenue account is emptied to the retained earnings account.

Working Out Your Final Trial Balance

The Final Trial Balance report details all the individual accounts of a business. Before this stage, all temporary accounts have been zeroed and converted to permanent accounts. The Final Trial Balance will also provide a summary of all permanent accounts that still have balances. In other words, the final balance-sheet trial report will only have balance-sheet accounts because you closed your revenue and expense accounts in the last phase. Also, the overall debits and credits have to align. Once they do, your general account balances are accurate, and you are 100% set for your next accounting cycle!

Reversing Your Entries

Reverse entries are journal entries created by the bookkeeper, and most commonly, the accountant at the outset of a bookkeeping process. It is an optional step in the bookkeeping process and can be skipped in most cases. These entries aim to reverse the changes made in the previous financial reporting period. This is usually used for income and expense accounts with accruals or prepayments in the previous accounting period.

When a reversing entry is not made, the accountant or the bookkeeper in charge must carefully recall the adjusting entries of the last cycle and then report them in the current period together with the revenues and expenses of the current cycle. Reversal entries will smooth the bookkeeping procedures for the bookkeeper because he does not have to recall the exact revenues and expenses that were accumulated and prepaid. This will document the reversing entries to counteract the impact of the adjusting entries that have been made in the previous year. The expenses and sales must be reported when they come in, and the bookkeeper will not have to think about the cumulative prepayments for the current period's last cycle.

If the bookkeeper does not report such reversals, he will have to recall the parts of the current expenditures already paid for in the preceding cycle. There is indeed a strong likelihood of double-counting some expenses and revenues. The process of creating reversal entries at the outset of an accounting process will ensure that this double- counting mistake is prevented.

Because most accounting is performed using accounting software, this procedure is also largely automated. When reporting an adjusting entry in the preceding year, the bookkeeper is expected to "mark" the entries as they are made. The accounting software will reverse these adjusting entries in the next accounting cycle; hence, the bookkeeper in charge doesn't have to worry about doing so.

Wrapping it Up

You can decide to close your books monthly or yearly, depending on your business type, goal, and objective. The procedures are the same; one involves closing the books monthly while the other involves closing your business books annually.

Once you've concluded every move and reviewed every part of your monthly/year-end rundown, you are good to go! Luckily, this method is made simpler if you are using accounting software.

Once you close your books or create a lock date, users may not be able to change or add transactions that happened before the closing date. Most of the time, the owner of the company will set a password so that only the administrator, accountants, and the bookkeepers can access past transactions. This lets your bookkeeper or accountant perform proper checks to ensure that the information recorded is up-to-date and, if necessary, make suitable corrections.

Conclusion

Small businesses crop up day in and day out, and only a tiny portion last to see their second anniversary, even though their business objective, goal, and the idea was a good one. Indeed, the difference between success and failure in today's business world is all about knowing how to crunch the numbers – this is precisely where bookkeeping comes in.

All those who managed to unlock the basics of bookkeeping, financial statements, and general basic accounting principles have been able to enhance their business growth; those who jumble through and only leave the numbers to the "numbers guys" always ruin their chances.

When viewed from afar, bookkeeping and general accounting principles seem intimidating, frustrating, and complicated. Some of it is, and that's the part that you should leave to the professionals.

Bookkeeping, among other accounting tasks, is critical for your business growth, especially for small business owners. This includes learning all that we have covered here, such as transaction recording, deciphering general ledgers, financial statements, and more.

When you have a good understanding of bookkeeping procedures and fundamental principles of accounting, you will be able to track and manage your organization's financial status.

Regardless of the size, every business is met with challenges and financial setbacks. Keeping your business afloat is hard; it's even harder to make steady profits. When you grasp how to use bookkeeping processes and accounting information to make informed guesses, you will be able to effectively get your business back on a more financially viable path. This is precisely how this book can help you!

When you've got a working knowledge of bookkeeping, from day-to-day transactions to structured financial statements, any problem can be addressed with numbers; and of course, these numbers must be recorded appropriately. In addition to understanding the fundamentals of bookkeeping and accounting principles, you will be able to reduce taxable income without lowering your earnings, increase cash flow without skipping payments to creditors, and use your company to build personal wealth. Besides, that's one of the key reasons you launched your business.

The bottom line: Just because you've completed this book doesn't mean that there's nothing new to discover about the subject of bookkeeping. Learning is continuous, and practice makes perfect!

Appendix: Bookkeeping and Accounting Terminology

Accelerated Depreciation: Accelerated depreciation is a depreciation technique whereby an asset drops its book value faster than the conventional straight-line technique. Typically, this approach allows for greater reductions of assets in earlier years and is used to reduce taxable income.

Account: An account is a database in an accounting system that monitors the financial actions of a specific asset, liability, equity, income, expenses, or other activities that may alter these resources and charges.

Account Payable: Accounts payable are the amount business owners owe creditors for delivered goods or services offered.

Accounts Receivable: These are claims against the debtor for unpaid bills, usually based on a successful transaction of sales or services delivered.

Accountant: The person who sorts and enters financial data into the accounting system.

Accounting: The method of collecting and recording financial data into a bookkeeping system. It also relates to finalizing the end of the year accounts, generating financial statements, and estimating tax payable by a certified practicing accountant.

Accounting Equation: The accounting equation is the basic accounting theory and a basic balance sheet feature. The equation is given as follows: Assets = Liabilities + Shareholder's Equity. This equation lays the basis for double-entry accounting and illustrates the layout of the balance sheet.

Accrual Accounting: Accrual accounting is an accounting method in which transactions are recorded as they occur, regardless of when the cash is exchanged. For example, if Mr. Smith purchases a book in February, and gets the bill in March, the accounting system used is an accrual accounting system. In the accounts, the purchase is documented and included on the Income Statement in February, on the billing date, rather than when it was paid in March.

Accrued Expenses: These are amounts owed by a company to its distributors or workers, which pertain to the current cycle but have not yet been invoiced.

Assets: Assets are those valuable items that are owned by a business. They are usually reported on the balance sheet and include current assets such as cash in bank accounts, cash in small cash boxes, accounts receivable, and non-current assets such as machinery, assets, and trucks.

Bad Debts: Those are sales invoices that have been written off specifically because payments are due and may never be paid. Sales invoices are only written off after some attempt has been made to recover the amount owed, often by debt collection agencies. Bad debts are usually expensed on the accounts.

Balance Sheet: The balance sheet report tells the owners and managers of the company the amount of equity they have in the company, the number of assets the business has, and what the business owes in debts. The balance sheet works hand in hand with the accounting equation.

Bank: A safe financial institution where business owners deposit their revenues and pay their debts. Banks offer financial strategies and also provide expansion loans to companies.

Bank Statement: A detailed printout of the balance in a bank account that displays the amounts deposited and withdrawn from the bank account, given to the owner of the account.

Billing: An invoice or other document obtained from a manufacturer, supplier, etc., typically for products or services received.

Bookkeeping: The process of collecting, documenting, and reporting financial transactions during a given period, usually monthly, quarterly, or yearly.

Bookkeeper: A qualified and experienced person whose duty is to perform financial reporting tasks.

Bookkeeping Cycle: A bookkeeping cycle is a looping procedure the bookkeeper follows when recording and reporting transactions. They are generally structured from the first day to the last day of the month and repeated monthly. During this period, bank reconciliations, financial reports, income tax, and payroll tax will be calculated. The end of the month is 'closed,' and the financial transactions for that month will not be altered in any way other than by trying to reverse/correct the journals, and that to be carried out only in the next month. This will continue until the end of the financial year when all data is submitted to the accountant in charge.

Budget: The financial plan where a company plans the amount it expects to accumulate in the coming year and what those projected earnings will be spent on and then compares/tracks the actual figures with the projected plan.

Capital: The personal funds the actual owner of business incorporates into a business.

Cash Accounting: Recognizes revenue and costs as they are paid or incurred, not when they are accumulated. This accounting system is the reverse of the accrual accounting system.

Cash book: The primary record that shows monies in and out of the business via the bank accounts. This report highlights the cash flow in and out of business and what it was spent on. Estimates will also be provided in the cash flow projections of profits and expenditure for the coming year. The estimates would be focused on actual profits and losses and will enable the company to meet its sales and budget objectives.

Chart of Accounts: This represents a quick outline of accounts set up in the accounting system where certain financial transactions are grouped. The main categories are as follows: Equity, Assets, Liabilities, Expenses, Cost of Goods, and Income.

Checks: Special pre-printed paper slips in a book format designed by your bank, used by a corporation rather than cash or internet banking to pay debts. Such notes are finalized by entering the date, the name or initials of the person/business getting paid, the amount in figures, and the value in words.

Closing Balance: The total and ultimate balance on the bank statement or in the ledgers account at the end of any specific day.

Cost of Goods Sold: Often recognized as cost of sales, this is the cost to the company of any part or stock sold to customers. This could also involve the cost of producing these goods.

Credits: Credits are located on the right-hand side of the double-entry bookkeeping system bookkeeping. A credit entry lessens assets and expenses and boosts income, liabilities, and equity.

Creditor: The person or company to whom the business owes money.

Debit: Debits are located on the left-hand side of a double-entry bookkeeping system. A debit entry boosts the assets and expenses of a business and lessens the liabilities, income, and equity.

Debtor: A client who owes money to your company.

Depreciation: Most assets closely related to a company drop in value over time due to wear and tear and everyday use – this is known as depreciation. The value that is used to depreciate the assets is measured with special rates, usually set by the tax department. It is given as the percentage of the cost price, less pre-calculated depreciation. Depreciation is often claimed as a business expense to lessen the income tax.

Double-Entry: The bookkeeping system whereby all financial transactions are recorded twice – once as a debit and the other as a credit. The debits must be equal to the credits. When they aren't, it is labeled as being out of balance. When this occurs, it implies that there is an error somewhere, and the error must be located and corrected.

Drawings: Funds withdrawn from the company by the owner of a business for personal use.

Entry: Every financial transaction recorded in a bookkeeping system.

Equity: Equity is a business's net assets or, in other words, assets less liabilities. The Equity category is listed on the Balance Sheet, which shows how much the company's owner allocated to the company through personal assets (capital) and how much they borrowed from the business for personal use (drawings).

Expenses: Most transactions made by a company are expressed as an expense. Expenses are often recorded on the profit and loss report and can be used to lessen the amount of tax owed to the government.

Filing: Filing is an act of putting away documents in a standardized way.

Financial Statement: Reports that are generated by a tax accountant at the close of a financial year focused on all the data entered into the bookkeeping system by the bookkeeper. Such reports reflect how well the company progresses, the company value, and are used to determine income tax that should be paid to the government.

Fiscal Year: A fiscal year is a financial year of 12 consecutive months, which can start from any month of the year.

Gross Profit: This is given as business income less the cost of sales; if the value is higher than the income, gross liability results.

Income: The amount earned by a business through product sales and services rendered.

Inventory: A compilation of products that a business buys and sells. Such products are stored, and a detailed record kept of the number of items on hand at a given period.

Invoice: A document outlining the sales or purchase of stock, parts, or services. The invoice shall contain necessary details, like date, invoice number, quantity, description, cost, total, and payment terms. Any time a business purchases products or services, it receives a purchase invoice, and when it sells goods or renders services, it provides a sales invoice to the customer.

Journal: An entry made to the accounts using a double-entry bookkeeping system to make changes to the accounts. It outlines the account debited and credited, the date, and the rationale behind the journal, accompanied by a reference.

Ledger: A ledger outlines all the entries made against the accounts, either as credits or debits.

Liabilities: The debt that the company owes to other businesses.

Loan: Funds, assets, or other material goods are given to a party, which ought to be paid back with interest or, in some cases, financial charges.

Loss: A loss occurs when the company's overall income is less than that of the expense that the company needs to pay to keep the business running. Typically, this is considered a net loss.

Net Profit: The result after deducting the business expenses from the gross profits.

Opening balance: The total amount in the company's account which is brought forward at the beginning of the accounting period.

Profit: The difference between the revenue made and the expense incurred.

Purchase: If a business buys goods and/or services, it is regarded as purchases.

Reconcile: The process of reconciling one set of figures or documents with another.

Recurring: A transaction that occurs regularly every week or month for the same amount at the same location is recurring or repetitive.

Salary: A salary is a fixed sum paid to an employee for his or her work. Salary earners do not earn extra pay like a wage earner when they work longer than regular hours.

Sales: All products or services offered to consumers fall under the category of sales.

Single-Entry: A bookkeeping system whereby all financial transactions are to be made only once. Normally, this is done in a cash book system that does not include journals and ledgers.

Wages: An hourly payment made to an employee in exchange for the work they do.

Withdrawal: This simply occurs when funds are taken out of a business or personal account.

Write-Off: This is commonly used by businesses that intend to account for outstanding receivables and loans, and in some cases, the cost incurred on stored business inventory.

Resources

12 Accounting Tools Every Small Business Needs. (2020, May 20). Retrieved May 18, 2020, from https://www.fundera.com/blog/accounting-tools

15 Reasons Why Bookkeeping Is Important for Your Small Business. (2019, July 30). Retrieved May 14, 2020, from https://lyfeaccounting.com/blog/bookkeeping-is-important/

Accounting Equation - Overview, Formula, and Examples. (2019, December 13). Retrieved May 19, 2020, from https://corporatefinanceinstitute.com/resources/knowledge/accounting/accounting-equation/

Accounting Terms. (n.d.). Retrieved May 20, 2020, from https://www.xero.com/us/resources/accounting-glossary/

AccountingCoach. (n.d.). Retrieved May 18, 2020, from https://www.accountingcoach.com/blog/equity,

Bookkeeping & Accounting Differences - Flatworld Solutions. (n.d.). Retrieved May 4, 2020, from https://www.flatworldsolutions.com/financial-services/differences-between-bookkeeping-accounting.php

Bookkeeping and Accounting: Difference, Process, Example. (2019, August 30). Retrieved May 3, 2020, from https://www.toppr.com/guides/accounting-and-auditing/theoretical-framework-of-accounting/bookkeeping-2/

Bookkeeping Terms and Basic Accounting Definitions. (n.d.). Retrieved May 20, 2020, from https://www.beginner-bookkeeping.com/bookkeeping-terms.html

Bragg, S. (2018, May 15). How to prepare an income statement. Retrieved May 19, 2020, from https://www.accountingtools.com/articles/how-to-prepare-an-income-statement.html

Cameron, A. (2020, March 13). How to Set up Accounting Books for Small Business | Getting Started. Retrieved May 18, 2020, from https://www.patriotsoftware.com/blog/accounting/how-to-set-up-accounting-books-for-small-business/

Cash vs. accrual accounting: What's best for your small business? (2019, May 3). Retrieved May 17, 2020, from https://quickbooks.intuit.com/r/bookkeeping/cash-vs-accrual-accounting-whats-best-small-business/

Closing Entry - Definition, Explanation, and Examples. (2019, September 10). Retrieved May 18, 2020, from https://corporatefinanceinstitute.com/resources/knowledge/accounting/closing-entry/

F. (2019, October 22). How to Close the Books: 8 Steps for Small Business Owners. Retrieved May 22, 2020, from https://www.freshbooks.com/hub/accounting/closing-books

Fishman, S. (2012, March 29). Bookkeeping and Accounting Basics. Retrieved May 8, 2020, from https://www.nolo.com/legal-encyclopedia/bookkeeping-accounting-basics-29653.html

Haughey, S. (2020, May 20). What is Bookkeeping? And Why Is It So Important? | ScaleBlog. Retrieved May 15, 2020, from https://scalefactor.com/scaleblog/what-is-bookkeeping/

How to Make a Balance Sheet for Accounting. (2020, March 23). Retrieved from https://www.wikihow.com/Make-a-Balance-Sheet-for-Accounting

How to Prepare An Income Statement: A Simple 10-Step Business Guide. (2020, March 20). Retrieved May 20, 2020, from https://www.freshbooks.com/hub/accounting/prepare-an-income-statement

Income Statement. (2013, February 15). Retrieved May 20, 2020, from https://financetrain.com/income-statement/

Income Statement - Definition, Explanation, and Examples. (2019, October 23). Retrieved May 21, 2020, from https://corporatefinanceinstitute.com/resources/knowledge/accounting/income-statement/

Income Statement - Definition, Explanation, and Examples. (2019, October 23). Retrieved May 19, 2020, from https://corporatefinanceinstitute.com/resources/knowledge/accounting/income-statement/

Learn the Basics of Closing Your Books. (n.d.). Retrieved May 19, 2020, from https://www.bizfilings.com/toolkit/research-topics/finance/basic-accounting/learn-the-basics-of-closing-your-books

Ledger Account Definition, Format, Types, and Example (Download). (2020, March 25). Retrieved May 21, 2020, from https://www.toppr.com/guides/fundamentals-of-accounting/books-of-prime-entry/ledger-accounts/

Nipu, Y. (2017, October 17). Double Entry Vs. Single Entry Accounting | Which One is Best! Retrieved May 18, 2020, from https://onlineaccountinghub.com/double-entry-vs-single-entry/

Reversing Entries. (2020, April 23). Retrieved May 20, 2020, from https://studyfinance.com/reversing-entries/

Small Biz Owner's Guide to Preparing an Income Statement. (2020, April 13). Retrieved May 19, 2020, from https://www.thebalancesmb.com/how-to-prepare-an-income-statement-393583

The Best Small Business Accounting Software for 2020. (2020, January 12). Retrieved May 16, 2020, from https://www.pcmag.com/picks/the-best-small-business-accounting-software

The Income Statement | Boundless Finance. (n.d.). Retrieved May 21, 2020, from https://courses.lumenlearning.com/boundless-finance/chapter/the-income-statement/

What Are Assets and Liabilities? A Simple Primer for Small Businesses. (2019, November 7). Retrieved May 19, 2020, from https://www.freshbooks.com/hub/accounting/assets-and-liabilities

What is the difference between cash book and cash flow statement - Accountancy - Cash Flow Statement - 13142977 | Meritnation.com. (n.d.). Retrieved May 18, 2020, from https://www.meritnation.com/ask-answer/question/what-is-the-difference-between-cash-book-and-cash-flow-state/cash-flow-statement/13142977

Part 2: LLC

What You Need to Know About Starting a Limited Liability Company along with Tips for Dealing with Bookkeeping, Accounting, and Taxes as a Small Business

Introduction

If you are one of the many highly motivated individuals who are looking to achieve the American dream by owning a business, forming a Limited Liability Company can be a great way to organize your company. This form of business structure has become one of the most popular in the U.S. because of its many advantages.

An LLC requires fewer formalities to start, protects you and your personal assets, and above all, offers tax flexibility. But don't take my word for it just yet. I will begin this book with an overview of the various business structures available to you and go over the main reasons an LLC is perhaps the best option. Whether you are just starting out as an entrepreneur or you have your own company established already, this book will help you understand why an LLC business may be the best option for you.

This book is divided into three sections for easy understanding and clarity. Part one contains in-depth information about the essentials of what a Limited Liability Company is and the various forms of LLC business structures available.

In part two, we zoom in on the process of forming a Limited Liability Company. If you are won over already on the idea of establishing your business as an LLC, this chapter contains a handy guide that takes you through the process. It will highlight the process of starting an LLC from scratch or converting an already-existing business to a Limited Liability Company. Part two also contains information about basic LLC formation processes, such as choosing the right name for your business, creating the articles of organization, and the LLC operating agreement, which is a vital document that establishes your business as an LLC.

This book is an A to Z guide on forming and running your own Limited Liability Company. Part three covers in detail the various processes involved in the day to day running of a Limited Liability Company. You will find information about how to do accounting for your LLC, preparing financial statements, and doing taxes for an LLC.

All the information contained in this book is designed to help you to build a Limited Liability Company that thrives and complies with all the regulations and standards. So whether your mind is already made up to start a Limited Liability Company or you still need some convincing, follow along as I show you, step-by-step, how easy creating your own Limited Liability Company can be.

SECTION ONE: LLC Business Essentials

Chapter One: What is an LLC?

For anyone planning to start a business, one of the major decisions they face is deciding on its organizational structure. This decision is important because the business structure will determine the income, liability implications, tax accounting, and other important details pertaining to the business.

Types of Business Structures

In the United States, there are four major business structures. They are sole proprietorship, partnership, corporation, and limited liability. We start by explaining each of these business structures as a simple guide to prospective business owners.

Sole Proprietorship

Most businesses that have just one owner typically start as a sole proprietorship. Many become nothing else. But many sole proprietorships grow and eventually become organized into other forms of business structures. Starting a business as a sole proprietor is a relatively simple process. You need not have any official government paper or have your company registered with the IRS. This is because a sole proprietorship isn't a taxable business entity. People who own a sole proprietorship simply need to add a profit and loss from business form (Schedule C form) to their personal tax returns, and they have things covered.

A sole proprietorship has the simplest business organization structure possible. This business structure gives total control of the company operations to the owner. Usually, they are home-based companies, small shops, one-person consulting firms, or simple retail businesses. A sole proprietor is responsible for the day to day running of the business. He or she handles activities like record-keeping, doing taxes (self-employment taxes), and decision making. This form of business structure provides no protection for the business owner. He or she is held liable for the company's financial obligations and debt.

Partnership

Any business started and ran by one or more persons is considered a partnership by the IRS. With a partnership, each person (partner) is considered equally liable. For businesses with more than one owner, a partnership is the most flexible structure you can go for.

Like sole proprietorships, partnerships are not taxable entities. Rather, each partner has to file his or her own income on their personal tax return and pay self-employment tax to the IRS. The partners also share joint liability. This means they are responsible for debts, financial obligations, and even for the actions of their partners in terms of the business. Partnerships can be formed simply through oral agreement and handshakes. However, a written legal agreement is the best option, as this will be helpful with lawsuits and disputes between partners.

Partnerships can be structured in two ways, either as a general partnership or limited partnership. In general partnerships, all partners pool their resources together to form the business, and they all participate in running the business. With limited partnerships, not all the partners participate in running the business. One partner actively takes control of business activities while the other(s) is or are only partners because of their financial contribution to the company.

Corporations

Corporations are businesses that operate as separate legal entities from their owners. Hence, the owners are protected from claims filed against the activities of the company or debts. However, the obligations of incorporating a company are enormous and significant resources will be required to pay for legal and accounting activities.

A corporation is the most complex form of organizational structure for any business. Typically, corporations are regulated by the laws of the state where they are set up. Unlike partnerships and a sole proprietorship, they are taxed as separate entities from the owner(s) by the IRS.

Corporations can be structured in two ways, either as S-corporations or C-corporations. This categorization is based on the way the corporations are organized in terms of taxation.

- S Corporation: Subchapter S corporations have less than 100 shareholders. They function more like partnerships because the income and loss of the company may be passed on to the shareholders to avoid paying federal taxes. However, the owners of the business have legal protection and are immune from corporate liabilities.
- Subchapter C Corporation: Ordinary corporations are regarded as subchapter C corporations. They are considered separate legal entities, and the tax returns are filed separately from shareholders. Because a C-corporation is a legal entity, in court it is treated more or less like a person.

Limited Liability Company (LLC)

A Limited Liability Company is a relatively new form of business structure. It falls somewhere in-between all the other business structures. It is organized in the form of a sole proprietorship or partnership but offers a level of legal protection similar to that of a corporation.

In most states, owners (members) of an LLC get legal protection from liability or lawsuits. They are not required to pay corporate taxes (unless they elect to do so) or go through every registration requirement of a corporation. They are essentially treated as sole proprietorship or partnership business unless they specifically request to be taxed as a corporation.

What is a Limited Liability Company?

Although it is the newest form of business structure, limited liability companies have become one of the most popular in the world. This is a sort of hybrid company. It combines the liability protection of an incorporated company with the tax advantages of a sole proprietorship or partnership business.

A Limited Liability Company is relatively easier to form compared to a corporation. The tax obligations flow down to the owners of the business (referred to as members in this case) who pay the taxes as personal taxes instead of corporate taxes.

The term "limited liability (LLC)" is used to refer to the specific form of private limited company practiced in the United States.

What is a limited company? In a limited company, the members bear a liability limited to their individual investment in the company. Limited companies are typically of two forms. They can be limited by guarantee or by shares. Limited companies limited by shares can be private or public companies. There are laws and rules in every country and state that govern who may become a member of a private limited company. But anyone can become a member of a public limited company by simply buying shares in the company. Although limited companies exist in different countries, each country has its own rules governing operation and organization.

Now that you are familiar with what a limited company is let's go back to our definition of a Limited Liability Company.

A Limited Liability Company combines the pass-through taxation structure of a sole proprietorship or partnership with the limited liability of a corporation. Under state laws, it is considered a corporation because the members are covered by limited liability. This business structure is well known for the flexibility it offers business owners to choose the tax rules under which the company will operate. An LLC may choose to operate under corporate tax rules where tax is charged in the form of corporate tax. They may also choose to be treated as partnerships with the tax charged as income tax for the members. In some cases, LLCs may even be organized as NPOs (Non-Profit Organizations.)

Although a common business structure, the limited liability structure is not open for all businesses. Companies that offer professional services that require state licenses may not be allowed to operate as LLCs. This includes companies offering legal or medical services. Such companies are only allowed to form a Professional Limited Liability Company, which is still similar to an LLC.

A Limited Liability Company is an unincorporated business. Hence, it is distinct from a corporation. Still, it shares a primary characteristic of a corporation in terms of limited liability. At the same time, it has the pass-through income taxation characteristics of a sole proprietorship (if it is owned by just one person) or that of a partnership (if it is owned by more than one person). Generally, operating an LLC is a more flexible form of business organization than a corporation. It is a business structure that is better suited to companies with one owner.

Besides the different tax laws governing both entities, LLCs and corporations are also described by different distinct terms. For instance, we don't say an LLC is "Incorporated" when it is formed. Rather, the term "organized" is used. Similarly, while the founding documents of a corporation are referred to as "Articles of Incorporation," those of an LLC are called "Articles of Organization."

Limited liability companies don't have "by-laws." Instead, the internal operations of the company are governed by an "operating agreement." The owners of the company are not called shareholders. They are members with membership interest or LLC interests measured in units or percentages (instead of shares). The legal document that represents the ownership right of members of a Limited Liability Company is known as a "membership".

Types of LLCs

The Limited Liability Company structure is one of the commonest business forms in the United States. LLCs can be structured in various ways, depending on various factors. Some of the most popular forms of organizing an LLC include:

1. Single-Member LLC/Multiple-Member LLC: As the name implies, a single-member Limited Liability Company is a type of LLC that is owned by an individual. Similarly, a multiple-member LLC is a type of LLC that is owned by more than one person. However, it is important to note that forming a single-member or multiple-member Limited Liability Company isn't only a function of the number of owners involved. A business owner will weigh the merits of each system to determine whether to form a single or multi-member LLC.

2. Member-Managed LLC/Manager-Managed LLC: A member-managed Limited Liability Company is run directly by the owner(s) of the business. In the manager-managed LLC structure, a separate manager will be appointed to manage the day-to-day operations of the business.

3. Domestic LLC/ Foreign LLC: Domestic Limited Liability Company refers to an LLC that operates within the state where it is registered. For instance, a company that is registered in Washington and does business in Washington is an example of a domestic LLC. Conversely, a foreign LLC is one that operates in a state outside of where it is registered. "Operating in" a state in this sense means:

- Having a bank account in a bank within the State
- Selling products in the State either directly or through parties directly tied to the company
- Owning property in the state (real estate, a fleet of trucks, etc.
- Having office facilities or holding meetings regularly in the state

4. Restricted LLCs: A restricted liability company is a type of LLC that has some restrictions within the Articles of Organization. Most notably, the members have to wait for ten years before they can receive their distributions from the business.

5. Anonymous LLC: As the name implies, an anonymous Limited Liability Company is an LLC where the details of the owners are kept private from the public. This is a very rare form of LLC.

LLCs may also be categorized based on how they elect to be taxed. An LLC may be taxed as a corporation or like a sole proprietorship. These and the other forms of limited liability companies will be covered in greater detail in chapter three, which will also cover some tips to help you choose the right business structure and options that suit your needs.

Chapter Two: Is an LLC Right for Me?

As a prospective business owner, before deciding to form a Limited Liability Company you need to be familiar with the various options available to you. You should also find out the advantages and disadvantages of a Limited Liability Company. This way, you can compare it with other forms of business structure and make a more informed decision. In this chapter, we will make a brief comparison of limited liability companies with other business entities, considering the specific advantages and disadvantages of each.

Limited liability Companies Compared to Corporations

The main similarity between limited liability companies and corporations is that both business types provide protection for their owners. Hence, this mode of business allows anyone to start a business without having to worry about liability. However, apart from these similarities, creating a Limited Liability Company also comes with some unique advantages over corporations. There are fewer corporate formalities involved in forming and running a Limited

Liability Company. An LLC also offers greater tax flexibility compared to corporations. It has some limitations, as well. Let's examine some of the advantages and limitations of LLCs compared to corporations.

Advantages of an LLC Over Corporations

1. Fewer Formalities: The process of creating a corporation is a very elaborate one; there are a lot of corporate formalities involved. Corporations are obligated to hold regular meetings among shareholders and directors. In these meetings, written records of discussions must be kept and submitted to the State as part of the annual reports. Without this documentation, or if they are not done properly, the "corporate veil" that protects shareholders may become invalidated in case of litigation.

This is not the case with LLCs. The members are not obligated to hold meetings. If they do hold meetings, they do so to keep the business running and not as a matter of obligation. This also means less paperwork is required.

2. Tax Flexibility: A Limited Liability Company is a pass-through tax entity by default. This means the default system of taxation is similar to that of a sole proprietorship or partnership, which helps to avoid double taxation. Only the owners of the company will be required to pay income tax while the company itself is free from any corporate tax liabilities. However, an LLC may choose to pay tax like a corporation.

3. Property Contributions: No matter how much interest an individual has in an LLC, the property contributed by him or her to form an LLC is not taxable. This is not the case with corporations. The IRS frees tax only on property contributors that have higher interest and control of the company, but the contribution of owners with minority interests are taxed.

4. There is No Restriction on Ownership: The membership of a Limited Liability Company can be made up of any number of individuals. But that of a Schedule S corporation is restricted to just a hundred. There is also no limit to the type of individuals the LLC can be made up of.

5. It Allows the Use of the Cash Accounting Method: Unlike C corporations that are only allowed to use the accrual method of accounting, LLCs are allowed to use the cash method of accounting if they choose to. What this means is that the company does not report income until payment has been received in cash, and tax is only paid on cash recorded.

6. Losses Can be Deducted: Managers of a Limited Liability Company can deduct the operating losses of the business from the regular income of the members to a certain legal extent. This may also be possible for some types of corporations, but it does not apply to all types. Shareholders in an S corporation can also deduct the operating losses of the business. However, in the case of a C corporation, this is not possible.

7. Membership Interests Can be Placed in a Living Trust: It is legally permitted for members of an LLC company to put their interests from the business into a living trust. This is not possible with an S corporation. Putting shares in a living trust, in this case, can jeopardize the status of the corporation.

Disadvantages of a Limited Liability Company Compared to a Corporation

1. Medicare and Social Security Taxes are Deducted from the Profits: For a Limited Liability Company that elects to be taxed as a pass-through tax entity, all the earned income of members will be subject to self-employment tax. This means deductions like Medicare taxes and social security taxes will be made from the earnings of the members. This might not be a problem for a big LLC where the members take out large salaries and profit. For instance, for owners with salaries and profits of around $120,000, social security taxation will not apply. However, in the case of a much smaller company, where the owner takes out about $30,000 as salary, and realizes profits of $20,000, up to $3000 will be charged as taxes.

In the case of a corporation, money can be taken either in the form of salary or as dividends, which will be tax-free. To avoid this, an LLC can choose to be taxed as a corporate entity instead.

2. Members of LLCs Must be Able to Recognize Profits Immediately: Again, this applies to LLCs that choose to pay tax like a pass-through entity. Since the profits are distributed automatically as part of the member's income, members will be taxed on the corporation's profits. This is not the case with corporations since the profits are not distributed to shareholders immediately.

3. Members Bear Personal Liability for their Payroll Taxes: If an LLC is taxed like a sole proprietorship or partnership, members of the company can be held liable if the company fails to pay payroll taxes. In the case of a corporate entity, the shareholders are not liable for failure to pay payroll taxes. Only officers and directors in the company will be held liable.

4. Unfavorable Tax Fees and Rules in Some U.S. States: Some states are notorious as regards tax rules for LLCs. They may require limited liability companies to pay more taxes on revenues than corporations are required to pay.

These are some of the advantages and limitations of LLCs compared to corporations. You must consider these merits and detriments when choosing between forming a Limited Liability Company or incorporating.

Next, we compare limited liability companies with sole proprietorship and general partnerships.

LLCs Compared to Sole Proprietorship

Limited liability companies offer even more advantages over partnerships and sole proprietorship. There is little wonder that most partnerships or one-man businesses switch to LLCs. But does that mean an LLC is always a better option? Well, there are instances where choosing to stay as a sole proprietorship business or partnership still makes more business sense. Let's consider the advantages and potential limitations of an LLC.

Advantages of an LLC over Sole Proprietorship

1. Limited Liability: This is, of course, the main advantage of a limited liability business over a one-man company or partnership. In the latter, the owner(s) of the business bear complete liability for the business. In cases of litigation, creditors are legally empowered to go after their assets and confiscate them. An LLC offers greater protection for members from such liabilities. Creditors cannot hold the bank accounts, real estate, or any other property of members of an LLC to pay for debts owed by the company. The only risk is with the initial investment contributed by the members into the business. The personal assets of the owners are not in any way affected in case of bankruptcy.

It is important to note that a Limited Liability Company cannot protect members who accrue debts through negligence or by standing as a guarantor for the company. Also, only LLCs formed and operated through the proper legal formalities such as filing of annual reports, keeping separate bank records, and so on will be protected under the law.

2. Continuous Existence: An LLC has a longer lifespan compared to a sole proprietorship or partnership. We could say that a Limited Liability Company has a perpetual lifespan. A sole-proprietorship's lifespan is virtually the same as that of its founder or partners. If they die, and the assets of the business are transferred to their heirs, that may very well be the end of the business, unless the heirs opt to continue it.

Even if the new owners decide to continue the business in their own names, it will be considered an entirely new business entity under the law even if they are making use of assets from the former business. This is because the new owners will have to get new licenses, register under a new name, and get new tax numbers, among other things. This is virtually the same as starting a new business from scratch. With an LLC, the business can still continue to operate with the former licenses even after the demise of a member.

3. LLCs are Easily Transferable: It is quite easy to transfer a Limited Liability Company, including all its assets and accounts to a new owner. This is done by simply assigning a stake in the company to the new owner. With a sole proprietorship or partnership, the process is much more elaborate. Assets, accounts, permits, and licenses must be transferred individually to the new owner.

For instance, if John decided to sell his Limited Liability Company to Jack, Jack does not have to apply for a new business license or change the titles on the real estate and other assets of the business. All of these are already in the company name and will remain the same, even if ownership of the business changes.

4. Profits Can be Shared Without Losing Ownership: For a sole proprietorship, sharing profits requires the owner to give up some control of the business. With an LLC, profit and ownership are separated. It is possible to set up a share of profit independent of the share of ownership on the business. For example, John, who is a member of an LLC, may assign a portion of his or her profit to his children. These children can be made members of the company, giving them a share of the company without actually allowing them control over the company.

5. Capital Can be Raised Easily: Another benefit of a Limited Liability Company over a single-owner business is the fact that capital can be raised easily through loans or by admitting new members into the company. In many cases, an LLC will not have to pay tax on money raised by selling part of the company's share. This, along with the fact that shares can be easily sold while the owners retain control of the business, makes it easy to raise money from willing investors.

However, the process of selling interests in an LLC is a thoroughly guarded one, with strict rules and serious punishments for violators.

6. Separate Record-Keeping: For a Limited Liability Company, the company's financial record and bank account are kept separate from those of the owner. This reduces the stress in differentiating between the expenses and other financial details of the business and those of the owner in a sole proprietorship.

7. Ease of Estate Planning: Given its similarities to a corporation, a Limited Liability Company is a more organized business entity. Hence ownership and management are better arranged compared to how it operates in partnerships or sole proprietorship. In the case of an LLC, members can be assigned percentages and given control individually. Members who are incapable or simply not interested in running the business can be exempted from management while still retaining their percentage of the profits. For instance, the owner of an LLC may decide to transfer the business to three members of his family. The person with the better business judgment can be appointed as manager of the company while the others simply earn a percentage of the profit without taking part in running the company.

8. Prestige: This is one of the little things that people seem to love about limited liability companies. The sound of "limited liability" seems a bit more prestigious than of "sole proprietor." For instance, which one do you think sounds more prestigious: "Acme Builders" or "Acme Builders, LCC"? The latter definitely sounds like a large, sophisticated company even though it is only a one-man operation that he runs out of his garage.

9. Separate Credit Rating: A Limited Liability Company is treated as a separate legal entity. This means that the company actually has its own credit rating independent of its owner's. This owner of an LLC can have a bad credit score, but this does not affect the company in any way.

Disadvantages of an LLC Compared to a Sole Proprietorship Business

Despite its advantages over a sole proprietorship or partnership, an LLC also has some disadvantages.

1. Cost: Operating a Limited Liability Company is slightly more expensive compared to a sole proprietorship or simple partnership. The startup cost is more similar to (or may even be slightly higher than) that of a corporation. A sole proprietorship business does not have to pay any annual fees or startup charges.

2. Taxes: Although a Limited Liability Company is more flexible in terms of taxation, it has some limitations as well. For instance, the owner of a Limited Liability Company may be required to pay unemployment compensation for himself. This is not necessary for a sole proprietorship.

3. Separate Records: Being a unique entity, the records of a Limited Liability Company must be kept separate from those of the owner. The owners of an LLC must keep their personal records apart from those of the company. Separate accounts must be maintained, and all monies received must be kept separate. This is both an advantage and a disadvantage. It means the owner or manager of the business has to go through extra stress to keep the records independent of each other.

LLCs Compared to Limited Partnerships

A limited partnership is a type of business entity owned by two groups of partners. One group (which can be one person or more) has control over the operations of the business. They are liable for the debts of the company. These are the general partners. The other group of partners only have investments in the company but do not participate in the management of the company. This means they are not liable for the debt of the business. These are referred to as limited partners.

Advantages of a Limited Liability Company Over a Limited Partnership

The main advantage of an LLC over a general partnership is that it provides liability protection for all the owners of the company. In a limited partnership, the general partners face the same liability concerns as a one-man business. Only the limited partners are free from this burden. An LLC offers equal protection for all members. Hence, there will be no need for general partners.

Additionally, an LLC also offers some unique tax advantages over a limited partnership. For example, it allows an increase in tax basis and passive losses. These provide the members with more deductions on their taxes. On the downside, the profits of a Limited Liability Company may still be subjected to Medicare taxes or social security taxes. These do not apply to a limited partnership.

Chapter Three: LLC Business Structures and Options

A Limited Liability Company is a very flexible business structure. This gives the owner(s) the freedom to configure the management and organization of the business as they deem fit. Some limited liability companies may be structured based on a specific professional service or organized in a way that takes advantage of some specific interstate commerce laws.

Types of LLCs

Although the legal structure of a Limited Liability Company is the same throughout the country, each state has unique rules governing its operation. Membership varies as well. An LLC may have just one member or several members. Here are the various types of limited liability companies.

Single-Member Limited Liability Company

Just like the name implies, a single-member LLC is owned by a single person. Hence, it is very similar to a sole proprietorship. The owner of the company is in charge of day to day company transactions. He is also responsible for doing the taxes and managing the company's debts. A single-member LLC may choose to be identified as a corporation or not. If the owner chooses not to be listed as a corporation, it will be classified as a "disregarded entity" under the law. In this case, the taxation is processed as a sole proprietorship. The single-member Limited Liability Company is the commonest type of Limited Liability Company. It is also the most affordable and requires less paperwork compared to other types.

General Partnership (Multiple Member LLC)

A Limited Liability Company can also be formed by multiple members. In this case, it will be referred to as a general partnership and all the members of the company will be in charge of the daily operation and transactions. They also take responsibility for the tax and debts of the business. Decision making in this kind of company is joint. Members have a say in when assets are purchased or sold. Each member will be required to pay taxes on their respective business income.

Family Limited Partnerships

This is the case when family members form a Limited Liability Company either as a single-member Limited Liability Company or as a general partnership. With a family limited partnership, members of the same families pool their assets to form the company. Hence, the family owns the business, but they can designate control to one member of the family.

Series LLC

This is a rare type of Limited Liability Company. In fact, only a few states in the US offer the option of a Series Limited Liability Company. A series LLC provides liability protection for members across multiple series. Each of these series is theoretically free from liabilities that may arise from the activities of other series. Each series are made up of business entities. The series may include members, managers, interests, and assets, each with their designated debts, rights, and obligations. Apart from Delaware, other states offering series LLC include Nevada, Illinois, Tennessee, Oklahoma, Iowa, Texas, and Utah. Each unit in the series LLC is taxed separately.

Restricted LLCs

The restricted Limited Liability Company is a new form of LLC that was introduced in 2009. Currently, it is only available in the state of Nevada. This form of Limited Liability Company is restricted by conditions in the articles of organization of the company. For instance, there is typically a ten-year waiting period before members of the LLC can start getting business distributions. This form of Limited Liability Company is also created under specific state rules in terms of the conditions for registration. These laws also set specific rules for the sales of the stock of such a company. There are also regulations that outline the voting power of shareholders, among other things.

The most significant feature of a restricted LLC is that the law allows a re-evaluation of the business worth based on a specific formula. This formula makes it possible to reduce the company's value based on new market value. This reduces the company's valuation discount. Consequently, the devalued company will pay lower taxes both at federal and state levels,

L3C Company

A low-profit Limited Liability Company is also known as an L3C. This type of LLC business entity is a bridge between non-profit and for-profit organizations. An L3C company provides a form of business structure that makes it possible for for-profit companies with socially beneficial programs to carry out charitable or social missions while still generating profits for its owners. An L3C company is typically established for philanthropic purposes, but the company also gets to enjoy the same tax benefits of conventional limited liability companies.

The main idea of this kind of business is to make it easy for companies to attract investment from charitable/philanthropic foundations and private investors. The Articles of Organization for forming for such a company and the tax requirement mirrors that of the traditional LLC system. This business structure is only available in a few U.S. states, namely Utah, Vermont, Louisiana, Rhode Island, Wyoming, and Maine.

Anonymous Limited Liability Company

An anonymous Limited Liability Company is just like any other regular Limited Liability Company. However, it offers an additional benefit of not disclosing the ownership information of the company to the public. This form of LLC is particularly desirable for companies who want to conduct their business with confidentiality.

Member-Managed LLC or Manager-Managed LLC

One of the core decisions in setting up an LLC is determining how the management will be structured. This and other details are usually specified in the operating agreement of the company. In terms of management, there are two main options. You can have a member-managed Limited Liability Company or a manager-managed LLC.

In the case of a member-managed Limited Liability Company, the day to day operation of the company is handled by the owners (members of the company). In this case, each of the members is authorized to act on behalf of the company. This is the more popular structure for the management of an LLC.

For a manager-managed LLC, an individual is appointed as a manager. He or she will be responsible for the daily operations of the company. The manager or managers will be specified in the company's operating agreement, with the consent of all the owners. Although the managers are usually appointed among the owners of the Limited Liability Company, they have rights and responsibilities different from that of the other owners. For example, the managers will have more voting rights, will be able to negotiate loans on behalf of the company, and handle operational tasks and financial affairs of the company. The non-managing owners of the company are free from all the obligations of operating the business.

The manager-managed approach is favored by companies with investors who typically prefer to remain as silent partners. This allows them to reap the reward of their investment without directly getting involved with the business. The fact that they are removed from the business also means they are less affected, and the business is more easily identified as a separate body when there are legal issues.

Domestic or Foreign LLC

A Limited Liability Company can also be domestic or foreign. This categorization is based on the state's laws under which the company is formed and where it operates. A Foreign Limited Liability Company is formed under the law of one state but does business in another state. In this case, the company will be subject to the laws of both states. However, the company will benefit from favorable tax laws and other laws in the state where it is formed. For instance, the state of Delaware is known for being quite favorable to businesses. You may choose to have your Limited Liability Company formed in Delaware despite operating in another state.

Key Considerations When Deciding Between a Single and Multi-Member LLC

1. Ownership: Although every state has their specific laws governing the creation of an LLC, the laws regarding ownership are quite similar in all states. Whether you are forming a single-member or multi-member LLC, ownership can include both citizens and non-citizens of the United States. Another corporation or LLC business may also form an LLC. As earlier explained, in the case of a single-member LLC, there is only one owner, and he or she has full control of the business. However, the LLC remains a legal entity on its own that is independent of the owner.

A Multi-member LLC, on the other hand, is owned by more than one member. They share control over the company. But the LLC is independent of its members. Members of the company may decide on how profit and losses will be shared among its members. The number of members that may form a multi-member LLC is unlimited. However, if you elect to have your LLC taxed as An S Corporation, the number of members cannot exceed 100.

The truth is, ownership is not a really important consideration in determining which type of LLC to form. Each of them have their own advantages and downsides. Some single business owners may find it more beneficial to switch to a multi-member LLC by simply making a spouse or relative a member. And in some cases, companies with multiple owners may opt for a single-member LLC. At the end of the day, it's all about individual preferences.

2. Management: A single-member limited liability company has only one owner who also acts as the manager of the business. In the case of a multi-member LLC, there are two options for managing the business. The members may opt for a member-managed system or a manager-managed system.

In the case of the member-managed business, all the members of the Limited Liability Company participate in managing the business. To make significant decisions like securing loans or entering a contract, there must be majority approval from all the members.

In the case of a manager-managed LLC business, the members appoint a member or members of the company to manage the business. A third party may also be appointed as a manager. The manager(s) has the authority to make decisions regarding the daily operation of the business. But the higher-level or strategic decisions of the company are still subject to the approval of all the members. But generally, they are only passive owners that only have financial interests in the company.

The member-managed system is the default arrangement recognized by state laws. If you want to form a manager-managed LLC, then it must be specified in the formation documents of the company. Regardless of the type of LLC that is being formed, the details must be specified in the operating agreement. This will ensure that all the members fully understand how the company will be operated. The operating agreement also includes the roles, responsibilities, and authority of each member. It also includes what happens if a member ends up leaving the company or dies.

3. Personal Asset Protection: There is really no difference in the level of personal asset protection offered by single-member and multi-member LLCs. No matter the management structure, the business remains a separate legal entity. Their personal properties are free from liabilities due to the activities of the business. In the event of legal disputes against the LLC, only the assets belonging to the company can be claimed. The members may lose their investment in the business, but nothing more.

However, there are situations where members may be held personally responsible for company issues. For instance, if a member participates in any illegal business activities or acts as a guarantor for a business loan for the company. In these cases, the personal properties of the member in question might be at risk.

3. Income Tax Treatment: A single-member Limited Liability Company is treated as a sole proprietorship in terms of federal taxes. Similarly, a multi-member company is treated as a partnership. The process of tax deductions is quite similar in either case. Unless the company elects to have it otherwise, the profits and losses of the business will be passed through to its owners. The owner of the business is expected to report this on the IRS Schedule C form 1040. The business will not have to pay any taxes as a separate entity. Additionally, the member(s) of the LLC will be required to pay self-employment taxes, which includes Medicare and social security taxes on all their taxable income from the business. These income taxes are estimated and paid quarterly. We will discuss how limited liability companies pay taxes in subsequent chapters of this book.

5. Compliance: Both single-member and multi-member limited liability companies have business compliance requirements. However, the process is generally less complex for a single-member LLC compared to multi-member LLCs. Following these compliance guidelines is important to maintain the personal liability protection that the members enjoy. Some of the tasks they need to follow include:

- Paying taxes and other fees

- Holding annual meetings, keeping minutes, and submitting annual reports
- Renewing licenses and permits
- Maintaining company records

There may also be additional compliance requirements depending on the state where the business operates. An LLC that violates these requirements may be fined, penalized, or have their business suspended. As expected, keeping up with these requirements is easier for a one-man Limited Liability Company since it is essentially a much smaller company compared to a multi-member company.

These are the major considerations that may influence your decision to form a multi-member or a single-member LLC. You can make a more informed decision by consulting with your attorney or trusted business advisor.

Chapter Four: LLC Taxes Explained

A Limited Liability Company is typically not recognized by the IRS as a business entity for taxation purposes. So, if you register your company as an LLC, how exactly will you pay your taxes?

According to the IRS, a multi-member Limited Liability Company may be treated as a partnership or corporation for the purpose of taxation. It may also be "disregarded" as a legal entity and treated independently of its owner if it is a one-member LLC.

So essentially, the way an LLC will pay taxes depends on whether it is registered as a single-member or multiple-member LLC. It also depends on if the LLC has elected to be treated as a separate taxable entity or not.

How does a single-member Limited Liability Company pay tax?

A single-member Limited Liability Company will be taxed like any sole proprietorship business. This type of business is treated as a disregarded entity. Basically, what this means is that the LLC and its owner(s) are considered separate entities. The owner, rather than the company, is taxed.

The implication of this is that all the company's profit and loss information will be filled into a Schedule C form. The net income calculated from this form will be brought into line twelve of the personal tax return for the business owner. This system is the default way of filing taxes for a one-member LLC.

How do multiple-member limited liability companies pay their income taxes?

Since a multiple-member LLC will have two or more members, the method used to prepare the income tax of this type of company is more similar to that of a partnership. Partnership businesses, like sole proprietorships, are not required to pay taxes to the IRS. Instead, each partner is required to pay their respective taxes based on their individual share of the company's profits.

The business is expected to file information returns using IRS form 1065. Subsequently, each member of the business will prepare a Schedule K-1 form. The gain or loss will be indicated on each member's 1040 form. Unless indicated otherwise, the IRS treats the taxation of any registered LLC this way. However, both single and multiple-member LLCs may elect to be classified as a corporation or as a pass-through business.

How income tax is filed for Limited liability companies classified as S corporations:

An LLC may choose to be treated as an S corporation only for taxation purposes. There are specific advantages of having your business classified this way. It is particularly favorable for businesses where the individual earns a higher income because they get to pay lower taxes.

An LLC company that opts to operate as an S corporation will follow these tax laws at the federal level and also pay state income tax. But the income of individual members is not taxed. The company will continue its operation as a Limited Liability Company in every other respect.

How do Limited Liability Companies that operate as pass-through businesses pay tax?

Limited Liability Companies that elect not to pay taxes as an S Corporations are referred to as pass-through businesses. This means that the business tax will be passed through to members of the company. It will be included as part of the income tax return for each individual, after each has received their share of the net income, based on the company's operating agreement.

For instance, consider a Limited Liability Company with 2 owners who share their profits equally. If the net profit of their business is $100,000, which is shared equally between them, then each owner will pay income tax on his or her share of $50,000. The income and loss from their Limited Liability Company will be considered together with the other incomes of the member from other businesses. This is their total tax liability. The profits from the Limited Liability Company will be considered as self-employment tax liability. However, if the company makes no profit within the tax period, then the member does not owe self-employment tax for that period.

Since tax flexibility is one of the major reasons most people create a Limited Liability Company, you should understand how LLC taxes are filed. This and other processes involved in running a Limited Liability Company will be covered in the next chapter.

SECTION TWO: Forming Your LLC

Chapter Five: Starting from Scratch or Converting?

Many small businesses start off either as a sole proprietorship or partnership. However, there might come a time when you, as a business owner, will need to legally expand the structure of your small business.

This decision can be due to different reasons. You might have noticed that your small business is getting bigger, and you are realizing that personal assets are at risk if your business were to be sued or go into debt.

In setting up a Limited Liability Company, there are two main options. For businesses just starting out with no prior registration, you need to follow the process of forming your LLC from scratch. It is also possible that corporations that have been in business for some years decide to convert to an LLC. In this case, you have the option of statutory conversion, statutory merger, or non-statutory conversion. This chapter will cover the process of forming an LLC, depending on which of these routes you are taking. We begin with how to form a Limited Liability Company from scratch.

Forming an LLC from Scratch – An Overview

Forming a limited liability from scratch is the same no matter the type of LLC you decide to create. There are only a few slight differences, depending on state regulations and other minor factors. We will cover this process in greater detail in this section. But first, here is a simple overview of the overall process of forming an LLC from scratch.

1. **Choosing a Business Name:** Like every business, one of the fundamental steps in forming an LLC is choosing a business name. You will need to search and verify if the name you have chosen is still available.

2. **Apply for an Employer** Identification Number (EIN): All limited liability companies are required to have an EIN. This is compulsory, whether you have hired employees yet or not. The EIN is issued for free by the IRS.

3. **Designate a Registration Agent:** All LLCs are required to appoint a registered agent. The registration agent will be in charge of receiving legal documents and notices from the IRS and other government bodies. The registered agent must have a physical residential address in the state where the business is registered.

4. **File Articles of Organization with the State**: This is the next crucial step in the process of creating an LLC. You will need to pay the filing fee and get the necessary document(s) in the State where the business is registered or in which it operates. The fees and information required may vary from state to state.

5. **Complete Entity Classification Election Form**: The next crucial step is to complete the IRS Form 8832. This form will determine the tax status of the LLC. A Limited Liability Company may opt to be taxed as a corporation or like a sole proprietorship business.

6. **Creating an Operating Agreement:** This is a set of documents that includes critical rules on how the LLC will operate. It is not a document required by states for registration, but this document is

vital for running an LLC. It will govern issues like how the authority will be designated among members, profit distribution, and dispute management, among other details. Even single-member limited liability companies need an operating agreement since the document helps to support the company's limited liability status.

7. Opening a Bank Account for your Business: Like a corporation, an LLC requires a dedicated bank account. This is an important step that helps to maintain the corporate veil of the business, ensuring the protection of the company members.

8. Obtaining Permits and Licenses: Aside from registering your business with the IRS and other relevant bodies, you also need to obtain special licenses and permits. This will allow you to conduct your business legally. The process for this depends on the type of business you operate and your location.

9. Learn the Employment and Hiring Requirement Laws: If your Limited Liability Company hires employees, then you must be familiar with various employment rules and abide by them. You may also be required to submit reports to the state, federal, or local government periodically.

This is a quick overview of all the steps you will need to follow to set up your Limited Liability Company. We will go into this in greater detail in subsequent chapters of this book.

In addition to all of these, you will also need information about the daily running of your business. One of such issues is taxation. Staying tax-compliant is important to maintain the corporate status of your LLC. In the next chapter, I will give a brief overview of LLC taxes. This will be discussed in greater detail in subsequent chapters.

Converting your Current Company to a Limited Liability Company

The alternative method for setting up a Limited Liability Company is to convert an existing business into an LLC. Typically, this process involves converting an already registered corporation into an LLC.

However, know that this is not an entirely straightforward process. Multiple factors can influence how this entire process goes, and can give rise to a wide range of scenarios. Some of the variable factors in the process of forming an LLC from an already existent company include:

- The Type of Corporation: As earlier explained in this book, there are two kinds of corporations: S schedule corporations and C corporations. C Corporations pay corporate taxes. S corporations, on the other hand, do not pay corporate taxes; instead, the shareholders are taxed through a pass-through taxation system.
- State Regulations: Corporations are allowed to be formed under one state's laws while operating in another state. This factor may be significant in the conversion process.
- Type of LLC to be Formed: Another factor that may affect the conversion process is the end product. Do you want your corporation to be converted to a single-member LLC or a multi-member LLC?
- Taxation: Taxation is usually one of the major motivations for converting a corporation into an LLC. It is only normal that it is an important consideration for forming your company. The newly formed LLC may be taxed as a partnership or a corporation or as a disregarded entity.
- Method of Conversion: Corporations can be converted to limited liability companies through statutory conversion, statutory merger, or non-statutory conversion.

As you can see, these variables will influence the conversion process one way or another. For instance, if you use the statutory merger method to convert an already existing C Corporation to a Limited Liability Company, so it can be taxed as a partnership, the process and paperwork will be different than that of the statutory conversion method to convert an S corporation to an LLC that will be taxed as a corporation.

The truth is, we cannot possibly cover every likely scenario that may arise here. But I will try to give a somewhat general overview of what this conversion process may entail. I'll try to simplify the process as much as possible. I will use one of the most common scenarios (converting a C corporation to a multi-member LLC) to explain the three methods of converting your company to an LLC.

Statutory Conversion

This is a relatively new procedure for converting an existing company into an LLC. This is a more streamlined and simpler process. However, it is not available in all states yet. Under this method, you can convert a corporation to an LLC by simply filing some forms at the office of the Secretary of State in the state where your company is registered. However, the process varies from state to state, and some states do not permit this process of conversion at all.

With this method, you can complete the process of converting your company in four simple steps:

- The directors of the corporation have to meet and approve the conversion.
- The directors create a plan for conversion then recommend the plan to the stakeholders who have to approve it.
- The conversion plan is put to a vote by the stakeholder. A majority vote is needed to proceed with the process.
- The directors can then proceed to file a certificate of conversion. The LLC certificate of formation and other needed documentation will also be filed with the office of the Secretary of State.

The implications of this process are straightforward. Once the statutory conversion process has been completed, the corporate stakeholders in the corporation become members of the newly formed LLC. This process is also quite straightforward in terms of asset transfer, and this is one of its advantages over other methods. The assets and liabilities of the corporation will be automatically transferred to the new LLC, as the old corporation no longer exists. With statutory conversion, all the processes are wrapped up into one. There is no need to set up a separate agreement for transferring stocks of members or their assets. No additional legal filings are required. Hence, the statutory conversion is not only faster but also cheaper than the other methods of conversion. If this is available in your state, then it is the most recommended option.

Statutory Merger

This one is a bit more complicated compared to the statutory conversion method. However, this is the next best thing, especially if your business is located in a state that does not have the option of statutory conversion available. Each state has its specific rules governing the process of the statutory merger, but the general process is essentially the same:

- A new Limited Liability Company is formed with the stakeholders in the corporation as members of the new Limited Liability Company.
- The stakeholders of the corporation must vote for a merger of their roles as members of the new LLC and stakeholders of the corporation.
- The stakeholders have to initiate a process that formally exchanges their shares for membership rights in the LLC.
- They must also file for a merger certificate and other legal documents from the office of the Secretary of State.

Just like the statutory conversion method, this method also legally transfers the liabilities and assets of the corporation to the newly formed LLC. However, before this transfer can take place, the new LLC must be formed as a separate entity first. This process involves several steps and additional fees. This makes the process of statutory merger more time consuming and expensive. Stakeholders also have to formally move to have their corporate shares changed to membership rights through the merger agreement (a process not needed in the case of statutory conversion). Many states also require the stakeholders to file for the dissolution of the corporation once the merger has been completed.

Non-Statutory Conversion

This is the most complex of the three methods of converting a corporation to an LLC. It is also a more expensive process, since there are a lot of steps involved. The steps involved include:

- Formation of a new Limited Liability Company
- The formal transfer of the assets & liabilities of the corporation to the LLC
- The formal exchange of stakeholder shares for membership rights in the newly formed LLC.
- Formal liquidation and dissolution of the corporation.

Unlike the other conversion methods, the non-statutory method of conversion does not automatically transfer the assets and liabilities of the corporation to the newly formed LLC. Instead, after forming the LLC, special agreements will have to be formulated to transfer these liabilities and assets. Additionally, special agreements will also be needed for the conversion of corporate shares to membership interests in the new company. Because the non-statutory conversion method tends to be more complicated, you may need legal assistance to get it done. Unless it is the only option available, this is not a recommended approach.

Before you go through the process of converting your corporation to an LLC, be sure to check the conversion and merger laws in your state. These tend to vary from state to state. For example, in California there is a conversion statute that makes it possible for corporations in the state to switch to an LLC structure by completing a form known as the LLC-1A. This form helps to simplify the process and skips some of the steps that are compulsory under the statutory merger or non-statutory conversion method. The state of Arizona has no conversion statue at all. Although corporations are allowed to merge into an LLC, they cannot simply change to a Limited Liability Company. This means the only options you get for converting your corporation into an LLC in Arizona are statutory merger and non-statutory conversion.

Important Tax Considerations for Conversion to an LLC

Perhaps the most complicated part of converting a corporation to a Limited Liability Company is working out the taxation rules for the new company. You must have this figured out before making the conversion since taxation is one of the major differences between the different types of business structures.

For example, if you convert from a C corporation to an LLC that elects to be taxed like a partnership, this will result in a larger tax bill. The corporation will be taxed along with the liquidation (transfer or sale) of its asset. The shareholders will also be taxed on any asset that is distributed among them. This will result in double taxation. Despite any factors that may affect the taxes, it is unlikely that any of the potential benefits of this conversion outweigh the cost of taxation.

If you are switching from a corporation to a Limited Liability Company that will still be taxed as a corporation, the adverse tax effects are a lot less than the scenario earlier described. The IRS can consider this conversion in either of these two ways:

- A straight exchange of stakeholder shares for LLC membership, which falls under IRC (internal revenue code) section 1036.
- An "F reorganization" that is largely tax-free.

However, although the tax bill is lower, the details of how the bill will be calculated may not be that straightforward, especially if it is treated as an F reorganization. Similarly, no matter how the IRS bills the taxation for the conversion, it does not affect how the business will pay taxes later on as an LLC. Hence, you must thoroughly investigate how this type of conversion will affect your company in terms of taxation.

You may also choose to convert your C Corporation to a Limited Liability Company that will be treated as a disregarded entity by the IRS. This is usually the case if you are converting a corporation to a single-member LLC or subsidiary of a larger corporation into a

Limited Liability Company. This system also applies if you are merging a corporation into a disregarded-entity that will be wholly owned by another corporation.

Each of these conversion options has its consequences as far as taxes are concerned. In the case of a single-owner LLC, for example, the conversion will be treated as if the old corporation is being liquidated, and associated taxes will be charged.

The examples treated so far refer specifically to conversion from a C corporation to a Limited Liability Company. The rules are slightly different for conversion that involve S corporations, especially in terms of taxation. An S corporation operates on a single level of taxation. The corporation itself is not taxed, but the shareholders have to pay taxes. Hence, the tax consequences of the conversion are limited compared to when a C corporation is involved. However, this advantage only applies to the conversion itself. Since both Limited liability companies and S corporations operate on a pass-through taxation basis, one has to wonder what advantages a business will gain from making such a conversion in the first place.

As you can see, the process of converting an existing business to a Limited Liability Company can be quite elaborate and complicated. You will also need an in-depth knowledge of the taxation rules involved both for the conversion itself and on the new LLC business when the conversion is complete. All these are important factors that must be carefully weighed before initiating the conversion process.

Chapter Six: Naming Your Company

The first and perhaps the most important step of creating a Limited Liability Company is choosing a business name. Not only important for the subsequent registration of your business and creating the articles of organization, a business name also serves legal and marketing purposes. Hence, choosing the right one is important. You want a business name that stands out and does a good job of communicating the products or services your business offers to people. You also want a name that is memorable, and easy to pronounce. But above all, your business name must meet all the legal naming requirements of a Limited Liability Company in your state of registration.

Considering all the many facets of choosing a business name, it is definitely worth spending your time and effort on the right name. Even though changing the name of your LLC later is quite possible, it will be best if you can get it right the first time. You don't want to waste all the brand recognition you have gained on a previous name when you have to change it in the future. Your LLC business name is something that you will hopefully use for a while, so putting in all the work now to get it right is not a bad idea.

So how do you go about choosing an LLC name? I will cover the most important considerations for choosing the right name for your company.

Brainstorm

The first thing to do is to brainstorm name ideas and produce a list of possible names. You can draw inspiration from your idea or concept of your business or personal sentiments. However, you cannot simply pick a great name out of thin air. You need to be creative with the process. Still, your creativity will best serve you when you put some helpful restrictions in place. You can produce a list of four to five names and choose the most fitting one based on the following considerations.

Is it legal?

Arguably the most important consideration in choosing a name for your Limited Liability Company is to ensure that it is legal. This will require you to be familiar with the list of required words that must be included and restricted words to be avoided in an LLC business name.

Adding a Limited Liability Company designation to your company is compulsory in almost every state. You can include the phrase "Limited Liability Company" or any other variation like "limited liability," "LLC," or "L.L.C" in the company name. For example, John & Sons LLC or Betty Lane Limited Liability Company. This is the only identifier that is made compulsory in all states.

States also have rules about words that *cannot* be included in the name of a Limited Liability Company. There are also restricted words that can only be used only in special conditions or with permission. For instance, words like "insurance" or "bank" are restricted words in most states. Some words are restricted to the naming of professional limited liability companies, and the process of registering such companies is different from regular LLCs. You should be able to find a list of restricted words or phrases for an LLC business name on the website of the Secretary of State in your state of registration. Be sure to include this in your consideration and strike out words or phrases that are non-compliant.

Branding Considerations for Choosing an LLC Name

Your Limited Liability Company is a brand offering a product for sale or selling a service. Therefore, you have to consider the branding implication of whatever name you finally settle on. You can find loads of material online that deal specifically with the subject of branding your business. However, here are some major considerations for branding your Limited Liability Company.

Make the Name Memorable

You want the name of your company to be one that people can easily remember. Whether you are using a play on words or an alliteration, choosing a memorable name will make it easier to keep your business in their minds. You don't want a potential customer or client to have trouble remembering the name of your business the next time they need your service or want to recommend your business to someone.

It is best to avoid acronyms and simply use names directly. It will cost you more in terms of marketing if you try to grab people's attention with a few letters. However, if you intend to shorten your business name, you can condense a longer name into an amalgam. For instance, Nabisco is the amalgam for the National Biscuit Company, while FedEx stands for Federal Express.

Longer names are often are usually more memorable than shorter names. So, you don't have to restrain yourself with the length of the name. You are also more likely to be able to find a unique domain name with a longer name than a short one.

Be Expansive & Global

One common mistake business owners make with naming is choosing a name that restrains their business to one location or niche. Unless you intend to create other versions of your business in other places, the name "Los Angeles Rentals" sounds pretty restrictive. You will have to rebrand or create a separate business if you decide to expand into other states in the future. Also, while choosing a niche is helpful, it is best to avoid tagging your name as specific to your business niche. That way, you will not be restricted if you decide to move your business forward. Unless, of course, your niche is a large one, and you have no plans whatsoever to expand into other areas in the future.

You should also try to make your business name internationally friendly. It would be bad to find out that your business name has a negative connotation in other cultures when you decide to expand your business abroad. For example, there is a brand of Toyota minivan with the name "Previa." Although this means "preview" in Spanish and Italian, in English, the words placenta previa refer to a condition where a baby's birth is obstructed by the placenta. Not a good name for a car, if you ask me!

Be Eternal

Some names sounded fashionable years ago but will sound completely outrageous today. Since most LLCs have a perpetual existence, try to choose a name that will sound good for many decades or centuries down the road. For instance, how does Twentieth Century Fox sound to you now that we're in the 21st century?

Make It Meaningful

You should choose a name that gives people an idea of what you are selling or the services you are offering. For example, the name "Jake and Dolly's Fascinating Whatzits" gives no clue whatsoever about what the company is selling. Being able to choose a name that gives people an idea of what to expect from your business is invaluable.

Careful here, though! When I say choose a meaningful name, I don't mean you have to give everything about your business away in its name. That is what tag lines and slogans are for. For example, choose between "Netflix" and "MoviesOnline" as business names.

The winner is obvious, isn't it? You still get a hint of what Netflix means, but MoviesOnline is a little too descriptive. Just make your company name as evocative as much as possible without giving out too much.

Be Original

The need for originality cannot be overemphasized. Although traditional trademark laws allow two firms to have similar names, newly introduced "anti-dilution laws" introduce some new challenges that you don't want to deal with. These laws make it possible for companies with "famous trademarks" to stop others from trying to do business with rip-offs of their name. So, while it may seem like a good idea to have a name that makes you sound like the big boys, you must steer clear of names that are already in use. Plus, you don't want your business sounding like a cheap rip-off when it really isn't.

The need for originality is even more important for internet-based businesses where you need originality to stand out from the competition. If your business name sounds too similar to another domain name, some of your traffic may end up going to that website.

Before you settle on a name, you should try to search for it to see what pops up. If there are too many results showing businesses with the same or similar names, you should change the name even if these businesses are not in the same physical location or serve the same niche as yours.

Generally, most states don't permit businesses to choose names that are confusingly similar to other businesses registered in the same state. In most cases, the state agency in charge of registration may offer a searchable online database of registered businesses in the state. You can use this database to conduct an LLC name search to confirm if the name you intend to choose is still available.

Marketing Considerations for Naming for your LLC

If your business name is not marketable, selling your product or service is most likely going to be difficult. There are several strategies that you will need to use to market your business. But if you choose an unfavorable business name, it will be difficult to make people recognize your brand and buy your products or services. Hence, before you choose an LLC name, think of the impact of the name on your marketing efforts.

Most marketing plans involve letting potential customers know about the services you offer. Think of how helpful choosing a name that aligns with the core values of your business will be. Try to tie one or two words together that are related to what you do or how you do business. This is a great creative standpoint from which to start thinking of your business name while keeping marketing in mind.

Keep it Simple

I know I mentioned earlier that longer names are more memorable. Still, a name that is too complex will hurt your marketing efforts. Keep the name short, simple, and easy to pronounce. You don't want people wondering if your business name is pronounced one way or another. If there is a simpler version of the name you have in mind, use it!

Make It Domain-Name Friendly

In this Internet-fueled era, choosing a name that is internet friendly is everything. Even if your business is not internet-based, you still need some form of online presence, usually in the form of a website. To set up a website, you need to choose a domain name. Even if you are not setting up a website immediately, check the business name register to see if the domain name associated with your business (or a very close variant of it) is still available. There is nothing worse than discovering there is no possible domain name available for your business after settling on a perfect name.

Also, some names may look good on paper, but terrible as a domain name. Take, for example, the name "Choose Spain"; it does not sound as bad as the name of a company selling lovely products from Spain. But when it is mashed together in a domain name like "choosespain.net," it doesn't look so good anymore. Since your website will most likely be the core of your marketing efforts, this is an important consideration.

Make It Social Media Friendly

Social media is another essential component of business marketing these days. Choosing a name that you can easily promote on social media is important. Just like the domain name search, you should check the major social media platforms like Facebook, Twitter, Instagram, and Pinterest for the availability (or close variants) of the name you intend to pick.

By putting all of these together, you should be able to come up with a great name for your business that not only meets the legal criteria but also sells your product and services effectively. Remember, that the LLC name isn't merely a means of identifying your business; your branding, and marketing efforts will be built on it as well. So, try to get it right and choose a name that is worth its weight in gold.

Chapter Seven: Creating Your Articles of Organization

Now that you have a cool and unique name picked out for your company, it's time to set the ball rolling and get down to the details of establishing your Limited Liability Company. Several steps have to be completed before you can achieve this, beginning with the creation of your articles of organization. Now, that probably sounds like some legal mumbo-jumbo. But creating your articles of organization is the most important step in the process of creating your Limited Liability Company. So, what exactly are the articles of organization?

What are the Articles of Organization?

The articles of organization of a Limited Liability Company are documents that act as a charter for the existence of a Limited Liability Company in any U.S. state. The articles also include some basic information about the newly formed LLC.

The articles of organization are filed together as a single document with the office of the Secretary of State or any state agency that is in charge of business registration. Basically, this document describes the basic operating characteristics and identifying details of the Limited

Liability Company. Filling this document and its consequent approval by the relevant state authority legally creates the LLC and seals its status as a registered company within that state.

An article of an organization is the legal document that creates an LLC. It is equivalent to the certificate of incorporation or articles of incorporation that you will need to file when you are forming a corporation. The Articles of an organization is a basic requirement for the formation of an LLC in all US states. However, it may be called other names in different states. For instance, states like Washington, Texas, New Hampshire, Mississippi, Maine, Delaware, and Alabama refer to it as the Certificate of Formation. It is called the Certificate of Organization in Utah, Pennsylvania, Massachusetts, Iowa, Idaho, and Connecticut.

The Process of Filing LLC Organizing Documents

Aside from the difference in name across various states, the information required for the creation of the articles of organization may also vary from one state to another. In this next section, we will go over, step-by-step, the process of creating the Articles of Organization for a Limited Liability Company. Note that there might be slight variations in your home state, but the general process highlighted here pretty much sums it up.

Step One: Check Secretary-of-State Website for your State

The first step in creating the articles of organization is to visit the website for the secretary of state or the relevant agency in charge of business registration in your specific state. Here, you will find all the information you need to create the articles of organization and all the items you need to include in your application. You should also find a detailed guide that works you through the process. Check to see if this form is available online or if you have to visit a physical location to file it. Typically, the filing cost for your articles of organization may be anywhere between $50 and $200. How much you will be charged also depends on your state.

Step Two: Gather the Information You Need for Filing

Before you proceed to fill out the form, there is some basic information you will be required to provide. It is best to collect all of this information beforehand. This will include information on the company itself as well as its owners.

Name of the Limited Liability Company: In the previous chapter, we already went over the process of picking a name for your company and important considerations for picking the right name. That stage of the process must be completed first before you can proceed to create articles of organization.

Once you have settled on a name, you are expected to carry out a business entity search to ensure its uniqueness. The name you put in your articles of organization is expected to include a "Limited Liability Company" designation or just "LLC." Some states do not allow the inclusion of certain words in an LLC business name. Words like "bank", "insurance", or "trust" cannot be included in an LLC name in many states.

Principal Place of Business: You will need to include the main location or headquarters of your company in the application form. The principal place of business is simply an address where the management of the company works or where company records are kept. The street address, not just the P.O. box, will be required for this. If you run the business from home, you can put down your home address as the principal place of business. In this case, your business will get a home-office tax deduction.

The Registered Agent: This is a requirement for the registration of an LLC (and pretty much all forms of business entities) in every US state. A registered agent is someone who sends and receives official paperwork on behalf of your business. He or she receives important legal documents from both state and federal agencies. A registered agent is also in charge of receiving service of process documents for your business. This includes legal documents like subpoenas or summons or any other form of notifications relating to a lawsuit. Registered agents are also known as statutory agents or agents of process. You may appoint an attorney, a corporate director, or a CPA to act as your registered agent. Some third-party agents perform this duty.

Although there is no rule that says you cannot act as your own registered agent, this is not common practice. Neither is it something I would recommend. A registered agent must be an individual that is available in one location to receive correspondence. It is unlikely that you will want to add this to the stress of running your company, which is why designating the duty to someone else is recommended.

The name and address of your designated registered agent will be included in your articles of organization as well as other public records. A simple search online should turn up some registered agents within your state.

Dates: another detail you will have to include on your Articles of Organization is the official launch date of your LLC. However, if there is no specific start date yet, you can simply use the date when the application was filed and accepted. Your state may also have specific rules about the date. You should check for this as well.

If the Limited Liability Company is expected to have a lifespan, then you can also state the specific duration through which the company is expected to last. However, since most LLCs last perpetually, most states do not make providing this information compulsory.

Organizational and Operational Details of your LLC: You will also be required to answer questions regarding the organization and operation of your LLC. Some of the details you may be required to provide include:

The Name of the Organizer: The organizer of a Limited Liability Company is someone that acts in order to form that LLC. This may be the owner(s) of the company or someone else.

Provide Professional Details: This is applicable for limited liability companies that will be providing a specific professional service. Such companies will have to specify this in the articles of organization. Businesses affected include those offering services like dentistry, chiropractic, law, medicine, public accounting, veterinary medicine, and psychology, among others.

Purpose: In some cases, you may be required to describe the purpose of the Limited Liability Company you want to form. The rules regarding this vary from state to state. For instance, in the State of Florida, LLCs that will be offering professional services must clearly state this in their statement of purpose. It should be written as "the practice of accounting, law, medicine...and so on," as the case may be. However, most states do not require a specific statement of purpose. Instead, a more general statement will be acceptable. For example, it may be written as "to engage in any lawful business for profit."

Management of the LLC: Another vital piece of information that must be included in the articles of organization is the LLC management details. We have already covered the two types of management structures of LLCs. You need to decide if the company will be member-managed or a manager will be appointed. Most states only require you to state which management format will be used, but some states may also require you to name specifically the manager designated for the business. Most limited liability companies are member-managed, which means everyone takes part in running the business. Some state laws will ask you to include the names and addresses of all the initial members of the LLC in the article of organization form.

Once you have filled in all the details above and completed the form accordingly, it should be signed by the authorized representative of the business. You can either mail the completed form along with the check for payment as specified on the website or submit it electronically. The procedure for submission should be specified on the Secretary of State website.

Additional information about creating the articles of organization:

As mentioned, most states require you to include a "Limited Liability Company" or "LLC" designation along with the name of the company. This is a compulsory requirement in most states. Since you are creating an LLC and not a corporation, do not use the term "Incorporated" or "Inc." for your Limited Liability Company.

Once you have completed the process of creating your articles of organization, there is no need to register the name of your business separately. The filing of the articles of organization is equivalent to registering your business name.

Although this is not a rule, you should use an official business checking account for the check. This will make your business look more legitimate. Although some banks will not allow you to create an account for your business until the articles of organization have been filed, most banks will.

You should keep a copy of the application form, whether in printed form or electronically, so you don't have to re-create it if it is needed in the future. In some states, you may be required to publish the articles of organization. For instance, in New York, a newly formed Limited Liability Company is required to publish a copy of the articles of organization or a notice of the formation of the company in two newspapers within 120 days of the approval of the articles.

Do You Need an Attorney for creating the Articles of Organization?

This is a matter of choice; there is really no rule concerning this. You can choose to complete the articles of the organization all by yourself or hire an attorney to complete the process for you. However, each state has its own rules for certain sections of the articles of organization. The process is best handled by someone who is more familiar with the rules and understands the process better.

What Next?

The articles of the organization officially create your Limited Liability Company. However, there are still some things that you have to check off your list before your company can begin operation. They may not be compulsory, but they are absolutely necessary for the smooth operation of your LLC.

Create an Operating Agreement

The operating agreement is similar to the by-laws of a corporation. This is a set of conditions that regulates the activities and operations of your limited liability company. It states how the business will be managed, how assets will be used, and how the revenues of the business will be shared among members. The operating agreement also specifies the rights and responsibilities of each member of the LLC. Some states have some default rules in the articles of organization, which may not be favorable to your business. The operating agreement effectively overrides these rules by describing exactly how your LLC will be operated. Hence, creating this agreement is quite important. In the next chapter, I will go explain the process of creating an operating agreement in greater detail.

Check the Annual Registration Requirements

To keep your business active, most states will require you to send in an annual or biennial report and pay a registration fee. You should look for the specific requirements for this process with your state authority. The purpose of this annual registration is to maintain an active status for your LLC and to provide current information about the management structure, business address, and other information about your LLC.

Obtain LLC Status in Other States

Although this is not compulsory, you can obtain an LLC status in other states outside your home state. This offers your company the same liability protection you enjoy in your home state in another state as well. It also makes your business look a lot more professional, which is quite attractive to prospective investors.

Run a Press Release

Once your LLC status has been approved, you may choose to run a press release in a local newspaper to announce the good news. This is a great way to attract attention to your business, draw in new clients, and get the attention of local investors who may be interested in your business.

Get an Employee Identification Number (EIN)

Even if you have yet to hire an employee for your business, you should get an Employee identification number. An EIN is compulsory if you intend to hire employees. Also, you can easily give your EIN to vendors or anyone else that needs it instead of giving out your social security number.

Obtain a Business Credit Card

If you do not have one already, I strongly recommend that you create a business bank account and get a business ID card to go with it. A business credit card will make it possible to track your purchases. This is especially important if you have employees or members that will have authority to purchase. This piece of documentation may also come in handy in case of litigation.

Acquire Business Insurance

While a Limited Liability Company provides personal protection for you against personal suits, getting business insurance will protect your business directly. If you can afford it, I recommend getting business insurance to cover potential damages, losses, or claims. Like all forms of insurance, getting business insurance will cost you. But in the long run, this may turn out to be less than the cost of not having it.

Chapter Eight: The LLC Operating Agreement

The Limited Liability Company operating agreement is a document that makes it possible to define the structure as well as the financial and working relationships of the co-owners (members) of a newly formed Limited Liability Company. It is the working document in which the operating guidelines of the LLC are stated. The operating agreement is the LLC equivalent of the articles of incorporation which govern the operation of a newly formed corporation.

Some of the details that must be included in the operating agreement include the company's statement of intent, the purpose of the business, the duration of the company's lifetime, and so on.

The operating agreement will also contain information about the membership of the business, their rights, and their responsibilities. Some of the membership details include the capital contributions of each member and their resultant share of the profit. It also itemizes how much control each person gets, how new members can join, and what happens in the event of the exit of a member.

As you can see, the operating agreement is a pretty detailed document. But is it compulsory to have one? Here are some of the reasons why you need to have an operating agreement for your Limited Liability Company.

Why You Need an Operating Agreement

In most states, an operating agreement is not a legal requirement for the creation of a Limited Liability Company. However, it would be quite unethical and unwise to try to run your Limited Liability Company without an operating agreement. While the details included in an operating agreement seem to be more relevant to a multi-member Limited Liability Company, you need to create one even if you are the sole owner of your LLC. This is because the operating agreement is pivotal to the maintenance of your company's limited liability status. In case of litigation, any form of mismanagement, or financial misunderstanding, you can refer to this document. It offers protection for members of the LLC against any personal liability.

While it may not seem like it, a sole proprietorship LLC needs an operating agreement just as much as a multiple-member company. Without the formality of this written agreement, your LLC is still very much like a sole proprietorship. The operating agreement will bring credence to the separate existence of your company as an entity before the law. This is the primary purpose of the operating agreement.

Other reasons why you may need an operating agreement include:

To Define the Management and Financial Structure of your LLC

This point is particularly relevant to LLCs owned by multiple members. The only document that contains the decision-making protocols and the profit-sharing plan for your LLC is an operating agreement. Without it, the co-owners of the company will not understand how the profits from the business will be shared and how management will be organized. This document also contains details of the process of admitting new members and how the departure of an existing member will be handled. These are issues that may cause problems between members of the company if the background rules are not properly set.

Overriding State Default Rules

Usually, every state will have laws governing the basic operation of a Limited Liability Company. These laws will most likely be included as default in the articles of organization (see the previous chapter). Although these default laws are not compulsory, the only valid way to override them is through the operating agreement, which allows you to set new rules upon which your company will operate.

For instance, in many states, the default rule for profit-sharing in a Limited Liability Company is for the profit to be shared equally among all members. This is not always practical. In many limited liability companies, investment sharing is based on the investment of each individual member in the business. As long as the co-owners did not invest an equal amount in the company, profit cannot be allocated equally.

However, without the operating agreement, the default rules stand. To override this default rule and others, you need to clearly indicate the terms of operation of your LLC in the operating agreement. The operating agreement makes it possible to set up your own rules and spell out the details of the inner workings of your Limited Liability Company. But what does this document contain, and how do you prepare one?

What to Include in Your Operating Agreement

An operating agreement is a highly detailed document that covers a whole range of issues regarding your Limited Liability Company. Most of these details are unique to your company, so you can't simply copy another LLC's operating agreement. Some of the details will depend on the specific situation of your company and the relationship between the business owners. Some of the most basic details that will be spelled out in an operating agreement include:

- The percentage of interest of each member in the LLC
- The rights and responsibilities of the owners
- Their voting power or authority on decision making
- Allocation of business profits and loss
- Management of the company
- Rules for meetings, note-taking, and decision making
- Management of cases of sale and purchase of interests and what happens upon the exit
  of a member.

It is expected that the operating agreement covers these major areas. Although all of these may seem simple and straightforward, they are major decisions regarding the company. There will be a need for rigorous and continuous coordination with members to reach consensus and spell out the terms of this agreement.

Basic Provisions of the Operating Agreement of a Limited Liability Company

While an operating agreement typically contains several important details, some basic provisions must be included. Any operating agreement for a Limited Liability Company (whether single or multiple-member) is expected to include these basic details:

Identifying Information

The operating agreement is expected to clearly identify the LLC. The identifying information includes the Limited Liability Company's registered name, the address of the registered office, and the business's principal operating officer.

The Statement of Intent

This statement indicates that the operating agreement is in accordance with the limited liability laws of the state. This statement also confirms that the business will come into existence when the official LLC documentation has been filed with the state authorities.

Statement of Business Purpose

This states the purpose of the limited liability company. It includes details like the nature of business and the product or services rendered. The Statement of Purpose may also include an additional general statement like "and for any other lawful business purpose." This statement helps to cover any changes in the business that may come up later.

Term

Most LLCs have a perpetual lifespan. If there is no specific end date in sight for your business, the operating agreement will indicate that the company will continue to exist unless dissolved according to state laws or the manner described in the operating agreement. For limited liability companies that are formed for a specific purpose and will only exist for a given period or until a specific event occurs, this should be included in the operating agreement as well.

Tax Treatment

The document must indicate how the company elects to be taxed. An LLC may pay tax as a sole proprietorship, as a partnership, or as a corporation.

Percentages of Ownership

In the case of a multi-member LLC, the members are people who have made financial or asset contributions to the business in exchange for a percentage of ownership of the Limited Liability Company. The operating agreement should indicate the percentage of ownership each member gets for their contribution. The default arrangement by state laws is equal membership rights among members. But in the operating agreement, ownership may be divided as the members see fit. Usually, the percentage of ownership will be determined based on the capital contributions of each member.

Admission of New Members

It is common for the membership of an LLC to increase with time. This agreement also outlines the process by which new members will be accepted into the company and how interests will be allocated. If this part of the agreement is not included from the start, you will have to create a new operating agreement that includes it if you finally decide to adopt members.

Other Provisions of the Operating Agreement

In addition to these basic provisions, the operating agreement of a Limited Liability Company may also include additional provisions. Some of these include details of the business or membership of the company itself, such as:

- Identification of Members and Managers: The operating agreement is expected to contain the names of all the initial business members along with their titles and addresses. If the LLC is manager-managed, the details of the managers should be included as well.
- Capital Contributions of Each Member: The operating agreement is also expected to include the initial capital contributed by each member. The capital may be in the form of cash, assets, or service rendered towards the company formation.
- Additional Capital Contributions: This applies more specifically to companies that have raised capital through additional contributions. If the members are not required to make any more contributions, this should be stated in the agreement. However, if an additional contribution is made, the interest percentage for each member's contribution should be included.
- Distribution of Profits and Losses: Usually, the distribution of profit and loss is based on the interest percentage of each business member. The specific format for this should be indicated in the agreement. The frequency of profit distribution should also be indicated in the agreement.
- Member Meetings and Voting Rights: For a multiple-member Limited Liability Company, you must indicate when and how meetings will take place. Details of the voting rights of

members and how votes will be taken should also be worked out among members and included in the agreement. For instance, it is important to state the minimum number of members that must be present to form a quorum and how many votes will be required to approve a decision. Members also have to decide if all the owners will get equal voting rights (I.e., one vote per person) or if the votes will be allocated based on the interest percentage of each member. Other relevant questions include if a unanimous or majority vote will be required to decide and the maximum or the minimum number of votes needed for a quorum, among other things.

- Management: One of the fundamental details of an LLC that must be determined beforehand is whether it will be member-managed or managed by a manager. If a manager is to be appointed, the agreement must state the process of electing a manager, the manager's tenure, and how much authority they have over the business. Typically, a manager gets to control daily operational decisions regarding the business, but major decisions are still subject to the approval of a quorum of members. The type of actions that will require the approval of the members will also be stated in the operating agreement.
- Responsibilities and Compensation of Members: If members of the company are required to perform any duties in operating the company, the agreement should state whether or not they get additional compensation for their services and how much they get.
- Admission or Withdrawal of Members: In later years, there may be a need to admit new members into the business. The operating agreement should indicate details of this process if there will be any. Also, if a member needs to withdraw or be expelled from the company, the document must indicate the procedure for this process.
- Transfer of Interest: If a member of the LLC decides to transfer his or her interest, the operating agreement has to provide a "right of first refusal" clause for the other members.

This gives the other members the right to buy-out the departing member's interests, based on the terms offered by a third-party buyer.

- Death of a Member: Another common provision of the operating agreement is what happens in the event of the death of an LLC member. There is a need to work out what becomes of the interests of such a member. The members may decide that the interest is automatically transferred to an heir of the dead member or if a first-refusal clause will be available for members to stop the transfer. Some agreements may also allow a transfer while giving the new transferee only rights to the profits but no controlling share on business decisions.

- Dissolution of the Business: Finally, the operating agreement is expected to highlight the conditions for the dissolution of the business and how it will be carried out if there is a need for it.

This sums up all the major provisions of the operating agreement of a Limited Liability Company. Although this is not an exhaustive list (since specific details of the agreement may vary from one company to the other), this is a general template that can be used to prepare the agreement. There may still be some additional legal and tax considerations that apply to your LLC agreement. You may wish to speak to a professional to have these additional details hammered out according to your needs.

SECTION THREE: Operating Your LLC

Chapter Nine: Setting Up Your LLC Accounting

Accounting is one of the essential skills needed by owners or managers of a Limited Liability Company. This is because accurate and comprehensive accounting is needed to preserve the limited liability status of the company. Proper record-keeping is needed to protect the personal assets of Limited Liability Company members from seizure to pay debts or settle legal disputes.

Skills like marketing, sales, and accounting are key administrative components of running a new LLC. By default, limited liability companies are not taxed as corporations, which makes them a popular choice for small business owners. They also require less record keeping compared to a corporation, yet they offer the same level of asset protection.

The bookkeeping requirements for a Limited Liability Company vary from state to state. For instance, some states require LLCs to file an annual report while others do not. But in most cases, keeping a comprehensive account of the daily business transactions is compulsory. Good knowledge of the taxation process is required. You don't want to run into trouble with the IRS. This is why you should seek the advice of a tax professional who can advise you on how an LCC is taxed, at both federal and state levels.

Do I Need a Business Bank Account for my LLC accounting?

Once the process of registering your new Limited Liability Company has been completed, you will need to open a separate bank account for your business. Some banks allow you to open business accounts even before the articles of organization have been approved. No matter the size of your new LLC and the membership structure, you are required by law to open a business account.

In choosing a bank to open your business account, some of the important considerations include the type of account that you need to open and what fees the bank charges to open a small business account. You will also need to know if the bank has branches or ATMs close to your business location or if you can bank online. There are two main types of business accounts you can open for your Limited Liability Company: a business checking account or a business savings account.

- Business Checking Account: a business checking account is used to receive payment from your customers or clients and to pay business expenses.
- Business Savings Account: you use this type of account to save a part of your business your income which will be used to make tax payments or ease the pains of the tax season. Money in your business savings account will come in handy in cases of emergency business expenses.

I also recommend getting a business credit card. Although not a type of bank account in itself, a business credit card can be used to build a good credit score for your business. You only need to ensure that you are paying up your balance in full at the end of every month. You can also earn cash-back and points for your business if you choose the right card, and you perform well on repayment.

Should I Keep My Personal and Business Finances Separate?

As the owner or member of limited liability, you *must* keep your personal finances completely separate from your business finances.

This is one of the primary reasons why a separate business account is needed for your LLC. Keeping personal finance separate from your business finance means you do not pay for any business expenses from your personal account or pay for personal expenses from the business account. Also, avoid transferring cash from your business accounts to your personal account for any reason.

Keeping your accounts separate this way will simplify your accounting process and make it a lot easier to do your taxes. Doing this will ensure that all your business expenses are in one place, and you don't have to sift through personal banking statements to track down your business expenses. It saves you a lot of stress and helps to keep things simple.

The General Ledger

The general ledge is the basic accounting tool for a Limited Liability Company and most of the other business types. A general ledger is similar to a checkbook in that it shows the day-to-day transactions of the company. Besides showing cash received or paid by the business, items like investment assets, valuable equipment, and real estate belonging to the business are also recorded in the general ledger. This document also details the loans, credit, and other liabilities of the business.

Keeping a comprehensive general ledger forms the core of business accounting for a Limited Liability Company. This document provides a detailed picture of all the financial transactions of the business. The information contained in your general ledger can also serve regulatory purposes, especially if you operate in a heavily regulated industry. Since the general ledger contains data for a comprehensive audit of your business activities, it will be a valuable document to show potential investors or buyers if you need to sell your business at some point in the future.

Choosing Tax Treatment

One of the most crucial aspects of setting up a comprehensive accounting system for your business is choosing the way your Limited Liability Company will pay tax. The decision on how the LLC will be taxed has to be made at the point of forming the company. A Limited Liability Company can elect to pay tax as a corporation or choose to pay pass-through tax like a sole proprietorship or partnership business. Even if you are using accounting software to handle your business accounting, you will be asked to indicate how your business entity will be taxed.

If the LLC members elect that the company will be taxed as a pass-through entity, they are required to pay employment taxes from their income at both federal and state levels. At the end of the business year, the owner of such an LLC must include a Schedule C form along with their federal income tax, or a Form 1065 in the case of a multi-member LLC that opts to pay tax as a partnership. For limited liability companies that elect to pay taxes as corporations, they need to fill the Form 1120.

Chapter Ten: Steps for Setting Up Accounting for an LLC

Once you have put in place all the fundamental considerations discussed so far, setting up accounts for your Limited Liability Company is straightforward and easy. First, you need to create a chart of your accounts. This is expected to include all the revenue that comes into the business and the expenses. You should also include the assets and liabilities of the business as well as the owner's equity accounts.

All transactions relating to the business must be recorded. This includes income received, equity withdrawn, written checks, and equity added; each of these is known as a "journal entry." If your journal entries are comprehensive and complete, you should be able to balance your accounts using the equation below.

Assets (A) = Liabilities (L) + Equity (E).

Accounting Methods

There are two fundamental accounting methods for a Limited Liability Company. You can choose to use the cash accounting method or the accrual method. Each of these has specific advantages and disadvantages.

The Cash Method

In this method, the record depends on whether cash has been received or paid out. You do not deduct expenses in your books until you have actually made a payment, and you do not add cash until payment has been received.

The Accrual Method

In this method, expenses and income are recorded the moment a sale occurs even if cash is yet to be received or paid out by the business. For instance, if you complete a project in January and send the client the invoice, but you don't get paid until June, you will record the payment in January when the invoice is sent. However, if you use the cash method, then the payment will only be recorded when you receive the payment in June.

The cash method of accounting is more favored by small business owners, largely due to its simplicity. The accrual method is slightly more complex. However, it paints a more accurate picture of the monthly revenue and expenses of a business.

Another advantage of the cash method is that it helps to delay taxes until you have the funds in hands. With the accrual method, you need to pay taxes of every transaction in the book even if you are yet to receive payment, but with the cash method, you will be taxed only on money that your business has received. Members of the LLC must decide on which accounting system will offer more benefit to the business, and this will be included in the company operating agreement. This lets the accounting staff know which method to use for tax preparation purposes.

The Accounting Cycle

Accounting for a Limited Liability Company follows the same accounting cycle as any other business. Transactions are recorded in journal entries as soon as they occur. Every entry is recorded according to the accounting method in use. Adjusting entries may also be made after the fact. These adjusting entries help to keep the accounts updated to ensure accuracy at the end of the accounting period. The accounting records are closed for the year after the adjusting entries have been made.

Just before closing the accounting books for the year, the accountant prepares the company financial statements, including the income statement, balance sheet, and statement of equity, based on the financial records. These first two records are the same for all types of limited liability, whether multi-member or owned by a single individual. The owner's equity statement must include each company member's investment in the case of a multiple-member LLC. This balance is then adjusted based on the income and loss and withdrawals of each member. We will discuss the process of creating financial statements in greater detail in the next chapter.

Choosing an Accounting System for your Business

There are several ways to organize accounting for your company. Although some people still make use of regular paper bookkeeping ledgers available for sale at office supply stores, more modern options are now available. There are electronic systems to organize accounting for your business. The most basic example includes simple spreadsheet programs like Excel. You can also opt for bookkeeping software like Expensify or QuickBooks, which come with specific features tailored towards making accounting easy for businesses.

Software designed for bookkeeping includes features that allow you to easily prepare income and expenditure reports for your business when you need to. Some of them also allow you to synchronize data from your bank accounts or merchant services that you use to receive payment, for more comprehensive accounting. This simplifies the entire accounting process. It also makes it easier to do your taxes since you simply transfer all the information to your tax adviser to get your year-end report and tax returns ready.

I wouldn't want to pitch any accounting software system as being the best. No matter what your choice, just choose a system that is regularly maintained. You also need a system that is simple to understand with no technical challenges. A system with lots of features is great, but you should take simplicity and effectiveness over systems with too many features that you rarely need.

Setting Up your Accounting System

Most standard accounting software has internal spreadsheets already included in the system. You will be prompted to complete the bank and vendor information as required. Even if you are using a manual paper spreadsheet, you should include a file tab that includes this account information. This way, you will not need other documents while working on your bookkeeping.

Bookkeeping software usually uses one ledger to keep payables and receivables. If you are working manually, you can decide to set up your records this way or not. While some people prefer to see all the running totals of their business, if you find extra columns of data overwhelming, then you should keep separate ledgers for payments and receipts. You should also include a column for client or supplier name, account number, date invoice was sent, payment date, and the expense category. This will make it easier to track transactions.

Also, if you are using one spreadsheet to track both the income and expenditures, you can enter income in one column and expenses in another. Then, the spreadsheet can be set up to deduct the expenses from the running balance of your system.

Other Bookkeeping Items

Besides tracking the income and expenses, which are the fundamental accounting details you need to track, there are other bookkeeping aspects you need to track as well. Some other bookkeeping items you should be familiar with include sales tracking systems, payroll expenses, and inventory.

A sales tracking spreadsheet helps to track information like the amount or quantity of items sold, their retail prices, and how much of the product was sold. It may also include the name of the person that made the sale. An inventory tracking spreadsheet makes it possible to track the number of products available in stock. Some electronic spreadsheets have all these features and can track and sync data across all these spreadsheets. For instance, when an item is recorded as sold in a sales spreadsheet, it is automatically deducted from the inventory. However, on some accounting software, you have to manually copy data across all the spreadsheets.

Setting up Payroll

Another essential part of bookkeeping for companies is setting up payroll. As a one-man Limited Liability Company, this might not be necessary. But as your business grows, you may need to hire contractors, freelancers, or even in-house staff to ease the workload. At this stage, your payroll will become a small but vital part of your accounting efforts. To do this, you will most likely need a payroll spreadsheet.

The essential part of this process is classifying your workers correctly. This is mostly for tax reasons. You may run into trouble with the IRS if you do not fill in your employee payroll correctly.

There are two main categories of workers. An employee is a worker hired by your business over whom you have financial and behavioral control. The company sets the working hours, work conditions, and duties of an employee. A contractor, on the other hand, is an independent worker. Payment for contractors is usually arranged on an hourly or project basis. Once you have your workers classified in this way, you need to be familiar with employment tax laws and put this into consideration in preparing your payroll.

How to Handle Accounting for your Business

As you can see, handling accounting for a Limited Liability Company can be a Herculean task. It involves tracking the business's day-to-day transactions, managing sales and purchases, assets, and liabilities. To do all of these well, you need to develop a working system to handle your accounting. There are three main options for this: you can choose to handle your accounting yourself, outsource the process to a third party, or hire an in-house accountant.

1. DIY Accounting: As a small LLC business just starting, doing accounting yourself is most likely the best option for you. As a one-man Limited Liability Company, you are probably going to be running all the aspects of the business yourself anyway. So, you might as well add accounting to the mix. You probably won't be earning enough to hire someone else anyway, and the volume of accounting should be small enough for you to handle yourself. A multi-member LLC may also have one member handling accounting as part of their responsibilities to the business.

2. Outsourcing: If no member of the LLC is good with numbers, or you simply have too much on your plate already, you can decide to outsource accounting. This can be in the form of hiring a freelancer or part-time bookkeeper. There are also several agencies offering online accounting and bookkeeping services.

3. Hire an In-House Accountant: As your business continues to grow and the workload becomes more difficult to handle on your own, you may hire an accountant in-house. This is the priciest option, but the most convenient of all if you can afford it.

Should I Hire a Small Business Accountant?

If you don't have enough time on your hand to handle your business finances, you may decide to hire an accountant to manage the process for you. In many cases, you may not need the accountant to oversee all aspects of your company finances, just the bookkeeping and report preparation. But even if you are not hiring an in-house accountant, it's a good idea to consult with an accountant for the accounting aspect of your business. Even before your business kicks off, an accountant can help you figure out the legal and financial structure of your business, the type of tax billing you should choose, how to file your tax returns, and so on.

Some of the aspects of your business an accountant can help you with include:

- Developing your financial strategy
- Preparation of financial reports
- Oversight of over-taxation planning and filing
- Ensuring that your business is tax compliant
- Negotiating business transactions and deals.

Wrapping Up

Good accounting habits and practices are vital to the success of your business. Keeping your records correctly and comprehensively will protect you from liabilities. You will also be a lot happier if you don't have to pay your tax preparer loads of money to comb through a box full of invoices and receipts in order to prepare your taxes. No matter the type of Limited Liability Company you are forming or the management structure you adopt, having a solid plan for accounting is super important.

Although laws regarding accounting and tax preparation may vary from one state to the other, all states require you to retain the records of all your transactions for at least three years. It is in your best interest that you comply with this and other accounting requirements. And if you don't know enough to handle it yourself, you should hire a professional to handle the process for you.

Chapter Eleven: Creating Your Financial Statements

Has your business succeeded or failed for the year? The annual financial statements are designed to answer that question. They provide a picture of your company's financial position for a fiscal year. Creating financial statements is one of the most important activities involved in managing a Limited Liability Company. Aside from its usefulness for planning the future of your business, financial statements are also important for tax purposes. In this chapter, I will explain various accounting terms associated with creating financial statements and go over the process of creating one.

What are the financial statements?

The financial statements of a company contain information about the operational results, financial position, and the organization's cash flow. The information contained in the financial statements is used to estimate the company's liquidity, funding, and debt position.

Annual financial statements are prepared for the public (in case of a publicly-traded company) but more specifically for taxation authorities who use the financial statement for the company's tax assessment. The statements are regulated by the IRS and the U.S. Securities and Exchange Commission. It summarizes the company's profits and losses and may also be used to calculate the company's income tax.

As a manager or owner of a Limited Liability Company, you are expected to file annual financial statements as part of your annual report for the company. For public companies, annual reports are available for any member of the public who requests it. For limited liability companies, you are required to file an annual report with the Secretary of State in your company's home state. This document is also made available for company shareholders, who can use the information in the statement to assess the security of their investments. Potential investors may also check financial statements before buying into the company.

Financial statements are also useful for internal communication. Since it provides an overview of the company's financial situation, it ensures transparency and accountability as it clearly shows how the company's capital was used. It can be used to measure the success or failure of a company's management. However, the results of the financial statement aren't the only thing that counts. A bad financial appraisal for the year does not always mean that the managers have done a terrible job. An in-depth look at the figures will reveal where the issues are and help in formulating a plan to plug these areas.

Who needs to prepare annual financial statements?

Publicly traded companies must prepare financial statements and make the details available to the public. Limited liability companies and corporations must also prepare financial statements and file them with the Secretary of State's office in the state where the company operates. Regulations for submitting financial statements and deadlines may vary from state to state. You must be familiar with the rules regarding financial statements in the state where your company operates. For sole proprietorships and simple partnerships, financial statements are not needed. A single income statement is usually all that you need to submit to tax authorities.

What makes up financial statements?

The financial statements of a company are expected to be a precise and comprehensive statement of a company's finances. For a Limited Liability Company, the two most important components of financial statements are the income statements and the balance sheet. Other documents that you need to include in the financial statements include a cash flow statement and a statement of changes in stockholder equity.

By comparing financial statements from various fiscal periods, it is possible to track the growth of a company. Although working on financial statements usually involves sitting down and assembling the related data into a specific format, in a real sense, the process of creating your financial statements begins with day to day bookkeeping. If you have been keeping comprehensive and accurate daily records, creating your financial statements will be as simple as pulling together all the information you already have. You will have trouble creating your financial statements if your books are incomplete. In this case, the process of creating your financial statements will have to begin by updating your books.

Now that you are familiar with what financial statements are, let's talk about the specific process of creating the various components of a financial statement.

Creating a Balance Sheet

The balance sheet is a summary of a company's financial situation for a given period. It lists everything a company owns, and everything it owes then calculates the difference between the figures to show the company's net worth.

To create a balance sheet for your Limited Liability Company, you need to list all your assets on the left side of the page. This includes everything your company owns, from the cash you have at hand to anything in your bank accounts. Your assets also include all your accounts receivable (what your customers owe you.) The values of equipment owned by the company and other assets must be estimated as well and added to the financial worth of the business.

One the right side of the balance sheet, the liabilities of the business are listed. This includes all the amounts the company is owing, including both short term and long-term debts. Credit card balances and bank loans should also be included in this part of the balance sheet. Accounts payable, unpaid supplies, and shipments already received are also part of the business liabilities.

The assets and liabilities are totaled separately. Then the liabilities are subtracted from the assets of the business. Whatever is left after subtracting the liabilities from the assets is the owner's equity. This is then added to the right side of the balance sheet. Once the owner's equity has been added to the liability column, you should be able to balance the balance sheet. This means the assets will be equal to your liabilities (at least on paper).

Steps for Preparing your Income Statement

To prepare the income statement for a Limited Liability Company, you must understand the individual components and know how to tie them all together.

1. Sales: This is a figure that represents how much revenue the business has generated for the period under consideration. The amount to be recorded in this section is the total figure for sales made minus sales discounts and any products returned.

2. Cost of Goods Sold: The cost of goods sold represents the direct costs of producing or acquiring the products you sell. This includes the cost of materials that were purchased from suppliers to be used for manufacturing the product. The internal expenses of your manufacturing process are added here.

3. For service businesses where no products are manufactured or purchased, the cost of goods sold will only include your expenses incurred in the process of supplying the service. If you own the company and you do not take additional salary beyond the

company's profits, then the service expenses will be zero. But, if you receive a salary from the business or you need to hire someone to offer the service, then labor costs will be added to the cost of goods sold section.

4. Gross Profit: To calculate the gross profit, you need to subtract the cost of goods sold from the sales. The income taxes and the operating expenses of the business are not included here.

5. Operating Expenses: Operating expenses are daily expenses that are incurred in the day-to-day operation of the business. They are in two broad categories: marketing costs and general or administrative expenses. Some of the possible operating expenses include:

- Sales Salaries: This includes the salaries, bonuses, or commissions paid to sales staff during the period under review
- Collateral and Promotion: These are expenses incurred by the business for the purchase or creation of sales materials used by the sales staff for business marketing. Promotions fees also include product samples or giveaways used for promotional purposes.
- Advertising: This includes the cost of multimedia advertisements for the company. This can be in terms of the cost of creating advertisement materials and the cost of placing the adverts.
- Other Sales Costs: You may include other costs associated with selling your products not covered in other sections here. This may include travel costs, client meals, cost of organizing sales meetings, and other miscellaneous costs.

Administrative Expenses

◆ **Office Salaries:** Salaries for part-time and full-time office workers

◆ **Rent:** Fee incurred on renting or leasing office, industrial, or warehouse space

◆ **Utilities:** This includes the cost of utilities like heating, electricity, internet services, phone usage, and so on.

◆ **Depreciation:** Depreciation refers to the loss in value of equipment owned by the company and used by the business. Assets and equipment belonging to a company that may become depreciated over time include computers, office buildings, furniture, and so on.

◆ **Other Overhead Costs:** Any other operating expenses that cannot fit into any of the other categories may be included here. Examples of such expenses are the cost of cleaning services, office supplies, insurance, and so on.

6. **Total Expenses:** Covers the total of all the expenses spent on running the business excluding interest or tax expenses

7. **Net Income before Taxes:** It represents how much the business has earned as income before income taxes are paid. You arrive at this figure by subtracting the total expenses from the company's gross profit.

8. **Taxes:** The income taxes owed by the business at Federal, state, or local levels are included here.

9. **Net Income:** The net income is how much the company has left after the income taxes have been paid.

Statement of Retained Earnings

The statement of retained earnings is also known as the statement of changes in equity. This statement forms an integral part of financial statements for corporations and limited liability companies. Although a statement of changes in equity is not required to prepare consolidated financial statements, its purpose is to show changes in equity between two fiscal periods.

The statement of retained earnings is expected to reflect all changes (whether upward or downward) in the company equity. The statement of equity changes provides context for the balance sheet using the content of the income statement. This statement is a requirement under the United States Generally Accepted Accounting Principles (US GAAP) in cases when the income statements and the comparative balance sheets are provided together.

Although there are no strict rules under commercial law on how this document should be structured, the statement of equity changes is expected to include the issued capital, capital reserve, retained earnings, annual profits, and the revaluation reserves. The information included in this statement is compiled from values from the previous year. It shows the key dates and events that led to the changes. At the end of the statement, the figures from the last key date and new figures should be displayed in the report. The result is a clear and concise table that shows all the changes in equity.

Cash Flow Statement

The cash flow statement should be included in any financial statement. Even if this statement is not compulsory, it is an important document, and it is recommended that you prepare it. The aim of preparing the cash flow statement is to indicate the cash flow between two reporting periods.

A cash flow statement shows the movement of all funds affecting a company's liquidity. This statement provides additional information about the flow of cash within a company, more than the income statement or balance sheet do.

Accounting is done through two major methods, i.e., through the accrual method or the cash accounting method. Most limited liability companies make use of the accrual method. In this case, the income statement in the yearly financial report does not represent the true cash position of the company. It is the cash flow statement that can truly reveal this since it focuses more on cash accounting.

Even though your business is profitable based on the income statement, you may still be failing in terms of cash flow management. For instance, a company that sells products on credit to its customers will record the sale as revenue even though cash has not been received. Consequently, you will need to pay income taxes on the profit on the items sold on credit based on the figures in the income statement. This is why the cash flow statement is important. It is a critical tool for analysts and investors in a business.

The cash flow statement has three components. They are:

Cash Flow from Operating Activities (CFO)

This is the first section of the cash flow statement. The cash flow from operations reports the flow of cash directly from the main business activities. This includes cash flow and outflows from activities like sales and purchases, employee payment, utilities, and so on. This section begins with the net income but then reconciles all the non-cash items relating to operational activities to the cash items. The cash flow from operations is essentially a statement of net income but in cash form. Generally, it is expected that a company can generate enough positive cash flow from its operational activities. If the cash flow generated is not sufficient enough, the company may need to seek financing from external sources for growth and expansion to be possible.

Cash Flow from Investment Activities (CFI)

The second section of a cash flow statement considers cash flows from the company's investments. It reports the cash flow as a result of gains or losses on investments. In this section, cash spent on property or equipment owned by the company is recorded. The main purpose of cash flow from the investing section is to track changes in capital expenditures. An increase in capital expenditure indicates a reduction in cash flow for this section. However, this isn't always a bad thing. An increase in capital expenditure could mean the company is making more investments into its future operations. High capital expenditure is usually an indicator of growth.

Although positive cash flow from investing can be good, many investors prefer companies that can generate adequate cash flow from their business operations directly.

Cash Flow from Financing Activities (CFF)

This is the final section of a cash flow statement. This section provides an overview of cash that is being used to finance the business. Typically, it measures cash flow between a company and its owners and creditors. The source of cash flow in this section is typically from equity or debt, while outflow can be because of loan repayment or dividends.

The cash flow from financing section is used by analysts to determine how much a company paid out through share buybacks or dividends. It can also be used to determine how the company raised cash to drive its operational growth.

Positive CFF indicates that more money is coming into the business than going out. Similarly, a negative figure could mean that the business is paying more debt or making dividend payments to shareholders.

Cash flow can be calculated through either direct or indirect methods.

The Direct Method

The direct method of preparing income statements involves calculating cash outflows and inflows directly from the cash flow of various business transactions. In this method, the cash flow is recorded directly based on the outgoing and incoming payments. The balance of these payments results in your cash flow statement. The items are marked according to their respective purposes.

The Indirect Method

This method involves deriving the information for cash flow statements from the annual financial statement. To do this, the income statement for all the non-cash transactions will have to be adjusted. The indirect method is only used for cash from the operating activities section. Cash flow from investing and financing is determined with the direct method.

Prepare Closing Entries to Get the Books Ready for the Next Accounting Period

After preparing your financial statement at the end of the fiscal year, there are still some simple tasks you need to complete. You need to prepare your accounts for the next accounting year. This involves preparing your closing entries by clearing out the expenses and income accounts in the general ledger then transferring the net income to the equity account.

Note that closing entries are quite different from adjusting entries. You need to adjust entries to update certain accounts in the general ledger at the end of a fiscal period. This is usually done before you begin to prepare your financial statement and your income tax return. Closing endings, on the other hand, is done to clear out income and expenses account at the start of a new accounting year.

Preparing your closing entries is a very straightforward process. Here are some tips to follow:

1. Close the Revenue Accounts: To do this, simply prepare a journal entry that debits all the revenue accounts. These accounts should have a credit balance in your general ledger before the closing entry. Prepare an account and call it "income summary," then credit it.

2. Close the Expense Account: Prepare another journal entry that credits the expense accounts. These accounts should be on a debit balance in your general ledger before you close the entry. Debit the income summary account for this total.

3. Transfer the Income Summary Balance to a Capital Account: For this, you will need to prepare a journal entry to clear out the income summary account. This entry will transfer the net income or loss of the business to the equity account.

4. Close the Drawing Account: If there is a drawing account, close it by preparing a journal entry that credits the accounts and debits the equity account.

Chapter Twelve: How to File Your Taxes as an LLC

As for filing taxes, a Limited Liability Company acts like a hermit crab. An LLC has no tax classification of its own. Like a hermit crab, it inhabits the tax home of other types of businesses. Limited liability companies can elect to be taxed like one-man businesses, partnerships, or corporations.

Although this tax flexibility is one thing that makes limited liability companies so appealing to business owners, the ever-changing nature of taxes for LLCs can be confusing for someone just starting. You must understand the differences between the various ways LLCs are taxed because the method of taxation can affect your total tax billing and your self-employment tax obligations.

How Are LLCs Taxed?

There is no specific tax classification for limited liability companies. The IRS has not established a unique classification for such companies. This means there is no dedicated LLC tax return form even though LLCs definitely have to pay taxes. To pay taxes, a Limited Liability Company can be treated as an entirely different entity. By default, a single-member LLC will be treated by the IRS like a sole-proprietorship while a multiple-member LLC is treated as a general partnership. However, every LLC can choose the preferred way they want to be taxed by filling a form with the IRS, which changes their tax status. The LLC may elect how it will be taxed at the time of its formation or make the election for tax classification at a later date.

Filing Tax Returns as a Single-Member LLC

For a single-member Limited Liability Company, the IRS treats your company as a sole proprietorship. In this case, the company itself is not taxed. Rather the owner of the LLC pays tax on his or her business profits like a sole proprietor does. You are expected to report your income and expenses on a Schedule C form, which is a personal tax return form. As the owner, you will also list the profit and loss of the business on the income section of your Form 1040, which is the U.S. Individual Income Tax Return form.

An LLC treated like a sole proprietorship is ignored for tax purposes. Such a company is also known as a "disregarded entity." The LLC still retains its limited liability status and only enjoys a " disregarded entity" status for tax purposes.

Multi-Member LLCs Taxed Like Partnerships

The IRS automatically treats a Limited Liability Company with more than one member as a partnership for tax purposes. In this case, the Limited Liability Company income will flow through to its members and will be reported on their personal tax returns.

But the company itself is not taxed. LLCs taxed as a partnership are expected to file Form 1065. This is an informational tax return form that reports the income and expenses of a partnership. The individual members of the Limited Liability Company are also issued a Schedule K-1 form. This indicates each member's share of the total profit of the LLC, per the company's operating agreement.

The LLC members also fill out a Schedule E form with their personal tax returns, reporting their share of the business profit or loss. Members are expected to report and pay taxes on their share of the business profits even if they decide to leave a percentage in the business as a form of reinvestment.

Self-Employment Taxes and Estimated Taxes

In the eyes of the IRS, members of limited liability companies taxed as partnerships or sole proprietorships are considered self-employed. For someone that works for an employer, the employer is expected to pay half of their Medicare and social security taxes while the employee pays the other half. But for self-employed individuals, the full amount must be paid by the individual since you are your own employer. However, while filing the annual tax return, a self-employed person is allowed to deduct half of the tax from their income. This helps to offset the impact of the self-employment tax in the long run.

You are expected to file a Schedule SE form with your tax return. This is a self-employment tax form that is used to report and calculate self-employment tax. You are also expected to make an estimated payment of these taxes along with your personal income taxes every quarter. You may be fined or penalized if you fail to do this when due.

LLC Taxed as S Corp. or C Corp

Besides the default system of taxation used for LLCs, a Limited Liability Company may also elect to be taxed as a corporation. Corporate taxation is not as straightforward as being taxed as a partnership or sole proprietorship. It is a good idea to consult with an accounting expert before choosing this system of taxation. LLCs that opt to be taxed as corporations may do so because:

- They intend to leave a substantial amount in the business every year as a way of financing future expansion plans.
- They want to minimize self-employment taxes because the company makes more profits than the amount the business owners should make in a salary.

To put this into effect, you are expected to file Form 8832 with the IRS; this is an Entity Classification Election form. When this is done, the IRS automatically treats the LLC as a C-corporation.

However, you can take things a bit further by electing to be taxed as an S corporation.

An LLC that elects to be taxed as a C corporation is expected to file a corporate tax return every year. The members of the company are also expected to report all their earnings in terms of salaries and dividends on their personal tax returns.

An LLC taxed as an S corporation follows a flow-through tax system. This system is similar to how partnerships pay tax. In this case, you are expected to file an information return and provide the company's members with a Schedule K-1 form which indicates their share of the business profits or loss. Each member is expected to report their income on Schedule E of the personal tax returns.

For small businesses that are just starting out, being taxed as a sole-proprietorship or partnership is the most recommended option. However, as your business grows, you may need to consult with an accounting expert to figure out the potential benefits of switching to corporate taxation for your LLC. In either case, you must know when and how to file an estimated annual tax form for your limited liability company to avoid being penalized or fined.

Should I File a Tax Return for an LLC With No Activity?

Sometimes, it is possible that your Limited Liability Company does not record any business activity for a business year. For instance, a newly formed LLC yet to start doing business or an older one that has become inactive but without formal dissolution. However, even if your Limited Liability Company is inactive for a year, which means there is no income or expenses for that year, you might still need to file a Federal income tax return. The requirements for filing tax returns for an inactive LLC depends largely on the system of taxation the LLC used. That is, whether you are being taxed as a corporation or treated as a disregarded entity.

Filing Requirements for Inactive Disregarded Entities

LLCs treated as partnerships or sole proprietorship are known as disregarded entities by the IRS. In this case, the income and expenses are reported as self-employment income by the members, and the taxes are paid accordingly. For a single-member company that reports no business activity for the year, there are no expenses to deduct. Hence, the members need not file a Schedule C to report the company income. However, the members will still need to file a personal tax return if he or she had another source of income within the period under review. In this case, a Schedule C will be filed for self-employment income from other businesses.

Filing Requirements for an inactive LLC Partnership

An LLC that is taxed as a partnership is treated the same way as other partnerships as far as federal income tax is concerned. Such a Limited Liability Company is expected to file an information partnership tax return unless it receives no income within a business year, and no expenses were recorded. In this case, there can be no claims of credits or deductions. So, unless there are expenses or credits the LLC wants to claim, it does not need to file a tax return.

LLC Tax Filing Requirements for an Inactive LLC Taxed as a Corporation

The rules for filing taxes for an inactive LLC being taxed as a corporation are slightly different from that of partnerships or sole proprietorships in the same situation. In the case of a corporation, you are expected to file a corporate tax return even if you have no income for the year. Hence, for LLCs that have elected to be taxed as corporations, you are expected to file a Federal income tax return even if the business was inactive throughout the year.

Even if your business is inactive during a business year, you are expected to understand how tax filing works for your company, so as to avoid fines and penalties.

Handling Tax-Deductibles for Limited Liability Companies

If you intend to start a Limited Liability Company, there are several expenses that you will have to cover on your own as part of the process of setting up your company. The good news, however, is that the IRS offers an opportunity for startups to claim tax deductions on business-startup expenses when they file their taxes each year.

According to the Federal tax code, owners of limited liability companies are allowed to deduct startup expenses and operational expenses that the business incurs before it becomes fully operational. This is applicable no matter the type of tax structure that the LLC adopts. But what exactly are these startup costs that businesses are allowed to claim deductibles on?

What Are Startup Costs?

Startup costs are expenses incurred by a startup in the early stages of its development. This includes costs like the money spent on creating the company, carrying out a market survey for your new business, marketing or promoting your new business, travel expenses, fees for training new employees, and so on. It essentially includes all the costs incurred before your first transaction with a client or customer.

The largest form of startup cost is organizational expenses. These are expenses involved in the registration process of a Limited Liability Company. They include attorneys' fees for drafting membership agreement and other costs relating to paperwork for the business. However, not all organizational expenses are tax-deductible; for example, costs of soliciting investors or attorney fees paid for drafting customer contracts, among others.

How Much Can You Deduct?

LLC members are allowed tax deductions on their startup and organizational expenses in the first year of the company's operation. The upper limit of deduction is $5000 of the LLC startup expenses. LLC members are allowed to make this deduction up to the amount of the total cost that is $50,000. Any cost that is over this amount is considered amortizable.

The startup cost deductions must be claimed on the LLC tax return in the same year the expenses were paid. For example, startup expenses for forming your company in 2019 must be deducted when you file your taxes with the IRS in 2020.

How to Amortize Startup Costs

Amortization is the process of spreading costs over multiple pay periods. Startup costs and organizational costs are classified as capital expenditures. Hence, they are subject to amortization rules. You can claim these deductions over 180 months beginning from the date the LLC becomes active. To amortize startup expenses, you need a 4562 Form, describing the company activities, which should be attached to your LLC tax return. You also need to attach a statement to the 4862 form which outlines the specific startup cost you want to amortize. You are expected to include the official date of the formation of your business along with your amortization request.

Conclusion

For filing taxes for limited liability companies, the process is a lot different from paying personal taxes. To avoid issues, you should consult with an accountant or LLC tax specialist to help figure out the best taxation system that will get you the most benefits, and also to find ways to save you money while keeping your business out of trouble with the tax authorities.

Chapter Thirteen: Setting Up Payroll and Paying Yourself

Congratulations! Now you have your Limited Liability Company fully set up and operational. Now, all you have to bother about is the day-to-day running of your business, which I must admit will be a handful. There are still a lot of things you have to do to keep your LLC running. One of those tasks is preparing payroll and paying your staff. In many cases, this also includes paying yourself as the owner of the Limited Liability Company.

Like everything else that involves your LLC, there is a process for this. Payroll for a limited liability company is not exactly the same as that of other business structures. The rules for paying yourself as the owner of an LLC are also different.

Owners of a Limited Liability Company are paid more like independent contractors working for the company than like regular employees of the business. If all the workers in an LLC are members (owners) of the company with no non-member working for the company, as far as the IRS is concerned, the company has no employees. In such a case, you need not prepare payroll or handle any payroll tax obligations. You only have to take on these responsibilities once you hire your first employee. The process of carrying out these tasks depends on the type of employees the company has.

Types of Employees in a Limited Liability Company

There are two broad categories of workers you can have in a Limited Liability Company. They can be non-member employees or member employees.

1. Member Employee: The members of the company are the owners of the Limited Liability Company. Members become part of the company mainly because of their financial investment, in terms of cash or assets. They hold membership interests in the company

2. Non-Member Employees: Non-member employees are people that are hired to work for the company, whether on a part-time or full-time basis. This group of employees is the ones commonly paid through payroll. A special group of non-member employees is contractors or freelancers hired to perform specific tasks for the company. Such contractors are not included in the payroll since they do not receive a regular payment from the company. Instead, contracts are paid via accounts payable.

Payroll Responsibilities of the Employer

An LLC that has employees on its payroll has some simple responsibilities to carry out regarding its employee payroll. These obligations are the same as those of other forms of business. They include:

- Withholding Federal, State, and Local Taxes on Behalf of the Employee: It is the responsibility of a limited liability company to withhold some percentage of the employee's wages as tax, which will then be paid to the government directly. The taxes withheld this way are deposited in bank accounts based on the IRS regulations.

- Filing a Tax Return Quarterly: The employers are expected to file a tax return and pay the withheld taxes to the government.
- Sending a Form W2 to Employees: As an employer, you are also expected to send the form W2 to your employees. This form summarizes the annual earnings of the employee and the taxes withheld.

Mandatory Employer Contribution

Under Federal laws, for every Limited Liability Company with employees, there are three mandatory benefits to which the business must contribute. These are the social security compensations, Medicare, and unemployment contribution.

- Social Security Benefits: Every company is expected to pay an additional 6.2% of the employee's salary for social security.
- Medicare Benefits: An employer is expected to pay up to 1.5% of an Employee's pay as a Medicare benefit contribution, plus an extra 0.9% for highly compensated individuals.
- Unemployment Compensation: Employers are expected to take full responsibility for the unemployment taxes of their employees. The employees make no contributions of their own to this payment. Only the business pays to the Federal Unemployment Tax Act through Federal Payroll Tax Contributions.

The LLC is expected to deposit these employer payroll taxes in the bank, along with the taxes withheld from each employee. The records for this are to be included in the quarterly tax return for the company.

Paying Yourself as the Owner of an LLC

Owners of an LLC business still have to earn a living. This is one of the main reasons you started your business. This means you have to know how to pay yourself from your LLC. There is a protocol for this, and you need to be familiar with it. There are two main ways you can pay yourself as the owner or member of an LLC. You can choose to be treated as an employee and receive wages from the business. You can also be treated as a member of an LLC. In this case, you receive distributions from the company profits. The process of filing taxes for either case varies.

Members Earning Wages as an LLC Employee

Owners of a Limited Liability Company are not considered employees of the company even if they work for the business. However, the company may provide compensation for services to the company in the form of guaranteed payment.

Paying yourself as an employee of your LLC means you earn compensation quite similar to a salary from the company regularly. This method of payment can be quite beneficial if you seek regular business income throughout the year. However, earning wages this way is not automatic; you must be offering your services to the business in one active capacity or the other. Members with no active responsibilities in the business cannot get paid through this method.

For multiple-member limited liability companies, if one member decides to take payment as an employee, all the members that participate in company operations must be paid this way too. However, if only one member has an active role in the business, then only that member will be paid through this method while the others will only get paid through distributions.

How Taxes are Paid for LLCs That Pay Members as Employees

All employee wages are recorded as part of the Limited Liability Company operating expenses and will be deducted from the company's total profits. However, you should be aware that the tax authorities will only permit reasonable wage deductions. Hence, the salary that members receive for their services to the company must be within the industry norms. In addition to the salaries, members that are also employees can also receive special bonuses for their services.

The W-4 form is filed with the IRS in order to determine how much will be withheld from your pay as payroll withholding tax. The company will pay your salary as a worker and will withhold the expected amount for your employment and income taxes from your salary.

Members that Receive Distributions from the LLC Profits

The second method of getting paid as an LLC member is to collect distributions from the yearly profits made by the LLC. Each member of the Limited Liability Company has a capital account based on their investment in the business. At the end of each business year, the company distributes the profits or losses into each member's account. Members can withdraw from their capital accounts based on the rules of the company's operating agreement.

So, if your Limited Liability Company posts a profit of $200,000 for a business year, and you own 50% of the company's interest, you are liable to receive $100,000 as distribution. For someone who prefers more consistent pay, you could have an arrangement that allows you to be paid ongoing payments against the expected profit at year-end. For example, if the expected profit at the end of the business year is $12,000, you can decide to withdraw $1000 monthly. At the end of the year, the total withdrawals you have made for the year will be removed from the total profit. You will also get any extra left after the deduction has been made. So, if the profit at the end of the year is $20,000, then you will get an additional $8000 at year-end.

How taxes are paid for LLCs that pay members through Distributions from LLC Profits.

For a single-member Limited Liability Company, you will not need to pay income taxes on the distributions you get. You will need to file a Schedule C form with the IRS to report the business profits along with your personal tax returns.

For multiple-member LLCs, the company is treated as a partnership. Each member of the company is expected to report their share of the profit, and they pay the income tax on this profit. A multi-member LLC has to file the IRS form 1065, which is used to report the profit or losses are shared among members.

Members of the LLC already pay tax on the money deposited in their capital account. Hence, distributions are typically not subject to self-employment tax. However, companies may not disguise their guaranteed payment as capital account distribution as a way to avoid the tax burden. Doing this would be illegal.

You should also note that it is possible to receive a monthly salary and also get the end of the year profit distributions. These two are not mutually exclusive. Members of an LLC offering their services to the company are eligible to get paid on both ends.

LLC Members Getting Paid Like Independent Contractors

Another way you, as the owner of a Limited Liability Company, can get paid is by working as an independent contractor for the company. In this case, you are not a regular employee, so you are not captured on the payroll. Instead, you will be paid like an independent contractor that does some work for the company.

For instance, you are the owner of an LLC but you also work independently as a graphics designer. If your company needs to produce some marketing or promotion materials, you may hire your own services as an independent contractor to produce the designs for the company.

But there are not so many benefits to this approach. You will need to file the Form W-9 with the LLC if you choose this method. And the LLC files a Form 1099-MISC at the end of the year. This will require you to pay the self-employment tax on any amount earned in this deal.

Aside from these three options, there is also the option of not receiving payment from the company at all and leaving all your profits in your business. However, in this case, you will still have to pay personal income tax on the total profit earned at the end of the year since the Limited Liability Company profit will be passed through to you on your personal tax return.

Conclusion

If you have made it this far, congratulations; you now know all that there is to know about forming a Limited Liability Company from scratch or converting your existing business to an LLC. Hopefully, you now understand the potential benefits of making such a move, and you can effectively distinguish between what you stand to gain from an LLC compared to other business structures.

The good thing about forming an LLC is the simplicity of the entire process. With this book, I have been able to simplify the process of forming and managing an LLC, along with describing all the tools you need. Of course, there are still some technical aspects of running an LLC that you may find a bit complex. For tasks like accounting, taxes, and even the process of setting up an LLC itself (creating articles of organization and operating agreement), you may have to consult with professionals in this field for further clarification. They will help provide first-hand information about how the process works.

Limited liability companies are probably the most popular form of corporate business structure right now. And for good reasons, too. Now that you have a better understanding of how to form this type of business works, all that's left is to decide to set up an LLC as your chosen business structure. Best of luck on your journey!!!

Here's another book by Robert McCarthy
that you might be interested in

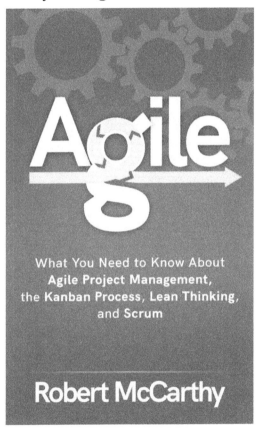

Glossary of Terms

Accrual Method of Accounting: In this method, expenses and income are recorded the moment a sale occurs even if cash is yet to be received or paid out by the business.

Articles of Organization: The articles of organization of a Limited Liability Company are documents that act as a charter for the existence of a Limited Liability Company in any U.S. state. It is filed with the office of the Secretary of State or any state agency that is in charge of business registration. Basically, this document describes the basic operating characteristics and identifying details of the Limited Liability Company. Filing this document and its consequent approval by the relevant state authority legally creates the LLC and seals its status as a registered company within that state.

Balance Sheet: The balance sheet is a summary of a company's financial situation for a given period. It lists everything a company owns and everything it owes, then calculates the difference between the figures to show the company's net worth.

Business Checking Account: A business checking account is used to receive payment from your customers or clients and to pay business expenses.

Business Savings Account: Using this type of account, a part of your business income can then be used for tax payments or to ease the pain of the tax season. Money in your business savings account will come in handy in cases of emergency business expenses.

Capital Account: The capital account records the individual accounting records of each individual member's investment. This balance is increased based on the initial investment of each member.

Capital Expenditure: This refers to the money a business spends on acquiring and maintaining fixed assets like land, buildings, equipment, and so on.

Cash Flow Statement: A cash flow statement shows the movement of all funds affecting a company's liquidity. This statement provides additional information about the flow of cash within a company more than the income statement and balance sheet do.

Cash Flow from Investing (CFI): The cash flow from investing reports the cash flow as a result of gains or losses on investments. In this section, cash spent on property or equipment owned by the company is recorded. The main purpose of cash flow from the investing section is to track changes in capital expenditures.

Cash Flow from Operations (CFO): The Cash flow from operations reports the flow of cash directly from the main business activities of the company. This includes cash flow and outflows from activities like sales and purchases, employee payment, utilities, and so on.

Cash Method of Accounting: In this method, the record depends on whether cash has been received or paid out. You do not deduct expenses in your books until you have actually made the payment, and you do not add cash until payment has been received.

Corporations: Corporations are businesses that operate as separate legal entities from their owners. Hence, the owners are protected from claims filed against the activities of the company or debts. A corporation is the most complex form of organizational structure for any business. Unlike partnerships and a sole proprietorship, they are taxed as separate entities from the owner by the IRS.

General Ledger: The general ledger is the basic accounting foundation for a Limited Liability Company and most of the other business types. A general ledger is similar to a checkbook in that it shows the day-to-day transactions of the company. In addition to showing cash received or paid by the business, investment assets, valuable equipment, and real estate belonging to the business are also recorded in the general ledger.

Limited Company: In a limited company, the liability borne by company members is limited to their investment in the company. Limited companies are typically of two forms. They can be limited by guarantee or by shares.

Limited Liability Company: A Limited Liability Company falls somewhere in-between all the other types of business structures. It is organized in the form of a sole proprietorship or general partnership but offers a level of legal protection similar to that of limited partnerships or corporations.

Limited Partnerships: A limited partnership is a type of business entity owned by two groups of partners. One group (which can be one person or more) has control over the business, and they are liable for the debt. These are the general partners. The other group of partners only have an investment in the company, but do not participate in the management.

Mandatory Employer Contributions: For every Limited Liability Company with employees, there are three mandatory benefits to which the business must contribute. These are the social security compensations, Medicare, and unemployment contribution.

Manager-Managed Limited Liability Company: In the manager-managed LLC structure, a separate manager will be appointed to manage the day-to-day operations of the business.

Member-Managed Limited Liability Company: A member-managed Limited Liability Company is run directly by the owner(s) of the business.

Multiple Member Limited Liability Company: a multiple-member LLC is a type of LLC that is owned by more than one person.

Non-Statutory Conversion: In this method of business conversion, a new company is formed, and the old company is merged into the newly formed one. Unlike the two other conversion methods, the non-statutory methods of conversion do not automatically transfer assets and liabilities of the corporation to the new LLC. Instead, after forming the LLC, special agreements will have to be formulated to transfer these liabilities and assets. Additionally, special agreements will also be needed for the conversion of corporate shares to membership interests in the new company.

Partnerships: Any business started and run by one or more persons is considered a partnership by the IRS. In the case of a partnership, each person (partner) is considered equally liable. Hence, they share the net profit, loss, and financial obligations of the business.

Registered Agent: A registered agent is someone who sends and receives official paperwork on behalf of a business. He or she receives important legal documents from both state and federal agencies. A registered agent is also in charge of receiving service of process documents for your business. Registered agents are also known as statutory agents or agents of process.

Restricted Limited Liability Company: A restricted liability company is a type of LLC that has some restrictions within the articles of the organization. Notably, the members have to wait ten years before they can receive their distributions from the business.

S Corporation: Subchapter S corporations have less than 100 shareholders. They function more like partnerships because the company's income and loss may be passed on to the shareholders to avoid paying federal taxes.

Series Limited Liability Company: A series LLC provides liability protection for members across multiple series. Each of these series is theoretically free from liabilities that may arise from the activities of other series. Each series comprises business entities that can include members, managers, interests, and assets, each with their designated debts, rights, and obligations.

Single-Member Limited Liability Company: As the names imply, a single-member Limited Liability Company is a type of LLC that is owned by an individual.

Sole Proprietorship: A sole proprietorship has the simplest business organization structure possible. It is a type of business owned and run by one individual. There is no legal distinction between a sole proprietor and the business entity he owns.

Statement of Retained Earnings: The statement of retained earnings is also known as the statement of changes in equity. This statement forms an integral part of financial statements for corporations and limited liability companies. Although a statement of changes in equity is not required to prepare consolidated financial statements, its purpose is to show changes in equity between two fiscal periods.

Statutory Conversion: This method involves filing a document with the secretary of state to change from one business-structure form to the other. With this method, there is no need to form a new entity. The company is converted to a different form entirely, and the assets, liabilities, and ownership interests are automatically transferred. This is the simplest and cheapest way of changing the form of a business entity.

Statutory Merger: This is a method of converting a corporation to a Limited Liability Company that involves an inter-entity merger. Under this approach, a new business entity is formed, and the old entity is then merged into the new one. With the statutory conversion method, the old business entity ceases to exist immediately; the process is completed. The liabilities and assets of the old entity are transferred to the new one.

Subchapter C Corporation: ordinary corporations are regarded as subchapter C corporations. They are considered separate legal entities, and the tax returns are filed separately from shareholders.

Common IRS Forms

Form 8832: This is an Entity Classification Election form. You must complete this form to elect the tax status of your LLC if it is not the assigned default status. You may take this form if you elect to have your company taxed as a C Corporation.

RS Form 2553: This is the "Election by a Small Business Corporation" form. You are required to file this form with the IRS if you wish to switch the status of your LLC from a C corporation to an S corporation for federal taxation purposes.

Form 1040: The IRS form 1040 is a tax form used to file personal income tax. This form is used to calculate a taxpayer's total taxable income and also determines how much the government refunds.

Form 1065: This is the return of partnership income form. All partnerships are expected to file form 1065, whether it is a general partnership, limited partnership, or a Limited Liability Company operating as a partnership.

Form 1120: This is the corporate income tax return form. Corporations use this form to report their income, losses, profits, and credit. Corporations or LLCs being taxed as Corporations use this form to figure out their tax liability.

Disregarded Entity: To report the taxes of your LLC as a disregarded entity, attach a single-member LLC tax form to your 1040:

- Schedule C, Profit or Loss from Business (Sole Proprietorship)
- Schedule C-EZ, Net Profit from Business (Sole Proprietorship)
- Schedule E, Supplemental Income and Loss
- Schedule F, Profit or Loss from Farming

LLCs classified as corporations file one of the following:

- Form 1120, U.S. Corporation Income Tax Return
- Form 1120S, U.S. Income Tax Return for an S Corporation

Schedule K-1 Form: This is an IRS tax form that is issued for investments in partnership. This form reports each partner's share of the profits or losses, either from the partnership business or an LLC taxed as a partnership.

Form W-3: This is the Transmittal of Wage and Tax Statements form. This is not a standalone form. It is filed alongside the Form W-2, and it summarizes the information contained in this form. It provides a compiled list of all the employee information that has been included in the Forms W-2. This form contains details like the amount paid to all employees, the total Federal income, mandatory contributions, and so on.

Form W-2: This is the Wage and Tax Statement. It reports the annual wages of employees in your company. The company is expected to send a copy of this form to its employees. The content of this form includes the wages paid to workers throughout the year. It also shows the gross wages and withheld taxes, among other details.

Form 4562: This is the Depreciation and Amortization tax form of the Internal Revenue Service (IRS). The purpose of this form is to make deductions for the depreciation or amortization of a piece of property.

CPSIA information can be obtained
at www.ICGtesting.com
Printed in the USA
LVHW080540261020
669798LV00006B/363